YORK NOTES

Gulliver's Travels
and A Modest Proposal

Jonathan Swift

Note by Richard Gravil

Longman   York Press

Richard Gravil is hereby identified as author of this work in accordance with Section 77 of the Copyright, Designs and Patents Act 1988

YORK PRESS
322 Old Brompton Road, London SW5 9JH

PEARSON EDUCATION LIMITED
Edinburgh Gate, Harlow,
Essex CM20 2JE, United Kingdom
Associated companies, branches and representatives throughout the world

First published 2001

ISBN 0–582–42476–3

Designed by Vicki Pacey
Phototypeset by Gem Graphics, Trenance, Mawgan Porth, Cornwall
Colour reproduction and film output by Spectrum Colour
Produced by Addison Wesley Longman China Limited, Hong Kong

CONTENTS

PART ONE

INTRODUCTION

HOW TO STUDY SWIFT'S TEXT

Studying on your own requires self-discipline and a carefully thought-out work plan in order to be effective.

- You will need to read each text more than once. Start by reading it quickly and for pleasure, then read it slowly and thoroughly. On your second reading, make detailed notes on the themes, imagery and recurring ideas.

- Although there are few true 'characters' in *Gulliver's Travels* there are recurring types – the wise ruler, the artful counsellor, the faithful friend – and it is useful to note the differences in Gulliver's relations with these.

- Make notes on whether Gulliver himself has any consistent characteristics. Does he develop from book to book, like the hero of a novel, or just change from page to page, as if he had no identity?

- Another thing to note is whether at particular moments you seem to be observing unfamiliar lands from an English point of view, or England from an alien point of view. Is there a difference?

- Note how often you have to revise your estimate of whether what Gulliver says is rational or irrational, moral or immoral.

- Cultivate the habit of finding and memorising several textual examples of each of the key themes, all the different kinds of irony and Swift's obsessions. You should also note the different styles employed for different purposes in both works, and be able to quote short and accurate examples.

- Finally, always express your own ideas in your own words.

This York Note offers an introduction to *Gulliver's Travels* and *A Modest Proposal* and cannot substitute for close reading of the text and the study of secondary sources.

Was Jonathan Swift a misanthrope or an idealist? Radical or Tory? A misogynist or champion of female education? Is *Gulliver's Travels* a merry work or an indulgence of spleen? Is *A Modest Proposal* the work of an Irish patriot or of a man contemptuous of all things Irish? One might expect scholars and biographers to agree on such questions, but with Swift there are no easy answers. In the late eighteenth and nineteenth centuries there grew a legend that *Gulliver's Travels* was the product of a lonely and bitter man, half crazed with anger at a world which had denied him success in Church or in politics, and writing his book as a kind of revenge. To the Victorians especially, with their optimistic view of human perfectibility and their pride in human achievements, the book was comprehensible only if one assumed that Swift was misanthropic to the point of insanity. The novelist Thackeray (1811–63) cautioned his readers against the fourth voyage in particular, which he found 'filthy in word, filthy in thought, furious, raging, obscene'.

Even in our century many readers have found it deeply disturbing. Aldous Huxley's novel *Brave New World* (1932) and George Orwell's *1984* (1949) can both be compared to *Gulliver's Travels* in the way they offer despairing visions of what the human race may come to, yet both writers were shocked by Swift's vision of what man actually is. Huxley found Swift guilty of hatred of mankind, basing his view on Gulliver's and Swift's obsession with excrement: 'Swift's greatness lies in the intensity, the almost insane violence of that "hatred of the bowels" which is the essence of his misanthropy, and which underlies the whole of his work'. Orwell, whose *1984* imagined a world divided into warring totalitarian blocs in which all liberties have perished, found Swift's concept of liberty disturbing. Despite the fact that 'Laputa' is clearly a **satire** on tyranny, and despite recognising Swift's contempt for absolutist authority, Orwell was disturbed by his feeling that Part IV is *recommending* a static totalitarian state.

These responses reveal something about *Gulliver's Travels*. There have been very few books which have left so many readers feeling that though the book is great there must have been something fundamentally wrong with the man who wrote it. His personality troubles them, and what he says about mankind disgusts or angers them. Swift himself *might* have taken a grim pleasure in such responses, for as he wrote to his friend Pope while revising the manuscript: 'the chief end I propose to myself in all my labours is to vex the world rather than divert it'. And in a later letter he added: 'I would *anger* it if I could with safety'.

In fact he seems to have failed with most people in his own day, for the book was a huge success immediately it was published. The first impression sold out in a week, and according to John Gay, who wrote to Swift a fortnight after publication, 'all agree in liking it extremely'. There were exceptions, of course. Lord Bolingbroke, Swift's Tory friend who had turned philosopher, was distressed at Swift's disparagement of human nature, while others felt that to criticise society too generally was to criticise the Creator.

Children, who generally read a cut version of the first two voyages, have no such problem. They have always been captivated by the adventures of Captain Gulliver in Lilliput and Brobdingnag. Swift tells the story with rapid strokes of narrative. There is no tedious psychology to cope with, and the descriptions are enlivened by wonderful comic invention of which the main effect is to convert everyday things into magical ones. Children are invariably pleased by the adventures of Gulliver the gentle giant in the toy-town of Lilliput, or of Gulliver in Brobdingnag, so shrunken that to him the larks are the size of sheep and a household cat is of dragon-like proportions. Children hold their breath while Gulliver holds an Emperor in his hand, or fights off an invasion of giant wasps, and – having recovered from these enjoyable frights – would no doubt agree with Dr Arbuthnot that 'Gulliver is a happy man that at his age can write such a merry work'.

One further response is worth looking at. Sarah Churchill, Duchess of Marlborough, whose famous husband, a national hero, suffered at Swift's hands more than anyone, was one of the book's earliest readers. According to John Gay the Duchess was 'in raptures' at *Gulliver's Travels,* and it taught her 'that her whole life hath been lost in caressing the worst part of mankind, and treating the best as her foes'. We need not take that too literally, but in her *Memoirs* she remarked that 'Dean Swift gives the most exact account of kings, ministers, bishops and the courts of justice that is possible to be writ'. Few people were better placed than the Duchess to know exactly what targets Swift had in mind. She could enjoy his clear-sightedness about backstairs intrigues and the malice of courtiers, and his willingness to strike out at corruption, cant and hypocrisy wherever he found it. And while she thought Swift mistaken in his alliances, she could admire the courage he displayed both in attacking the most powerful men of the age, and in defending his friends more valiantly than they deserved.

So one can see this book in many lights: as the ravings of a lunatic misanthrope, a merry work, an austere religious critique of man, or an 'exact account' – an insider's account – of the follies of the establishment. We know enough about Swift to dismiss the first of these views fairly confidently. Swift, in the years he wrote *Gulliver's Travels,* was in full possession of his faculties. He enjoyed the friendship and esteem of the wittiest celebrities in England and Ireland. He was so far from being an embittered recluse that he knew himself to be a national hero, in Ireland at least, for both *Gulliver's Travels* and *A Modest Proposal* belong to the decade in which he devoted his skills most fruitfully to the cause of improving the situation of Ireland. He wrote with savage indignation, certainly, but impelled by a moral passion that is hard to distinguish from the most ardent philanthropy, however abnormal its expression may be.

So it is wise to be on our guard against those who project their own negativity onto Swift himself. What Swift himself says is ambivalent, as we must expect in a habitual **ironist** – perhaps the greatest ironist in English literature, and certainly the greatest **satirist** – but it is fairly clear that his anger is usually reserved for those who mislead, rather than those who are misled. As he wrote in *Some Free Thoughts upon the Present State of Affairs* (1714): 'God hath given the Bulk of Mankind a Capacity to understand Reason when it is fairly offered; and by Reason they would easily be governed, if it were left to their choice'. His work is not an attack on the common person, but on those who, corrupted by their passions or self-interest, misuse their reason to deceive and enslave others. His keen eye for cant and hypocrisy, and his lacerating attacks on pride and pomp, intrigue and exploitation, colonialism and warfare, neglect and cruelty, have ensured that the works of this sometimes bigoted and intolerant Tory have been loved by rebels of all political complexions, in each generation from his own day to ours.

PART TWO

SUMMARIES & COMMENTARIES

Some parts of the first two voyages of *Gulliver's Travels* may have been written as early as 1714, but Swift began in earnest in 1721. He finished Parts I and II in the following year, wrote Part IV in 1723, and Part III in 1724–5 (while also engaged with the Drapier's Letters). In 1725 he revised the whole work and it was published on 28 October 1726 by Benjamin Motte who, according to Pope, had received the manuscript only two months before, knowing neither 'from whence, nor from whom, dropped at his house in the dark from a hackney coach'. Although Swift knew that publishing **satire** was a risky business, he was angered by the first edition, in which the printer had made a number of alterations and omissions. Charles Ford, a friend who had arranged the original publication to preserve Swift's anonymity, then made a list of corrections which were printed in the revised edition of 1727. A further edition, containing numerous corrections was published by Faulkner in Dublin in 1735. This York Note is based on *Gulliver's Travels*, edited by Peter Dixon and John Chalker, and introduced by Michael Foot (Penguin Books, 1967). This follows Motte's 1726 text but incorporates corrections supplied by Ford and by Faulkner. The notes on *A Modest Proposal* (1729) are based on *A Modest Proposal and other Satirical Works* (New York: Dover Publications, 1996). Two more expensive selected editions, containing both texts, are listed under Further Reading.

SYNOPSIS OF *GULLIVER'S TRAVELS*

In appearance *Gulliver's Travels* is the sole work of Captain Lemuel Gulliver, an educated seafaring man who has set down his memoirs of four voyages to remote countries of the world as a contribution to human knowledge. In reality it is the masterpiece of Jonathan Swift: an elaborate concoction of political **allegory**, moral fable, social **anatomy**, **Utopia** and

Dystopia, set within a skilful parody of both travel fiction and journals of scientific exploration.

In his first voyage, to Lilliput, Gulliver is shipwrecked on an unknown island near Sumatra and wakes to find himself the captive of a race of people six inches tall. As he describes the history and customs of these people, they seem remarkably similar, at times, to the English. In the satirical pattern of the work, Part I presents a detailed political allegory of the reigns of Queen Anne and George I of England. Not for a moment does Gulliver cease to be Gulliver, yet his services to the state and his near impeachment for treason bear a curious resemblance to the experiences of the Earl of Oxford and Viscount Bolingbroke.

In Part II, Gulliver is accidentally abandoned by his shipmates in an unmapped region of North America where the inhabitants are twelve times his size. Here Gulliver is adopted as a pet, and exhibited as a freak of nature. Both scale and plot are reversed. Brobdingnag, unlike Lilliput, bears little resemblance to England, but the political **theme** is continued, with Gulliver as a representative eighteenth-century Englishman attempting to justify the human race under the gentle interrogation of a benevolent giant king.

Part III opens with Gulliver captured by pirates and abandoned to his fate near some small islands in the vicinity of Japan. He is taken aboard the flying island of Laputa, inhabited by people who are obsessed by abstract sciences and speculations, yet are able, by their superior position, to tyrannise the land of Balnibarbi beneath them. That we are back in the ill-governed Britain of George I is soon apparent, for Part III is full of contemporary detail. But the satire is now less political than intellectual, examining man's claims to be a rational creature by showing us numerous examples of how man abuses his reasoning powers. From Balnibarbi Gulliver makes an excursion to Glubbdubdrib, the island of Sorcerers, where his host allows him to hold conversations with the moral giants of ancient history, the 'immortals' of Western culture. But if he is under any illusion that real immortality would improve humankind his next excursion, to Luggnagg, disillusions him. Here he meets the race of Struldbruggs, fated to everlasting senility, the most mortifying sight he has ever beheld.

Part IV completes the satirical argument by creating a **Utopia** of pure reason and measuring man against this impossible standard. On his first voyage as Captain he is the victim of a mutiny. Abandoned on shore, he encounters a noble race of horses, the Houyhnhnms, and their 'cattle', the Yahoos. Despite their human shape, Gulliver finds the Yahoos the most 'disagreeable animal' he has encountered in all his travels. By contrast the Houyhnhnms appear to be 'the perfection of nature' and Gulliver comes to love their way of life. The grace and dignity of the philosopher-horses is all the more effective for being preceded in the *Travels* by a succession of humanoid races, the absurd and spiteful Lilliputians, the grotesque Brobdingnagians and the intellectual freaks of Part III. But the Houyhnhnms regard Gulliver as a kind of Yahoo, a view which he is forced to share. Exiled from the land of these 'inimitable' beings, Gulliver returns unwillingly to England, where he divides his time between talking to his horses and attempting to 'reform the Yahoo race in this kingdom'.

So Gulliver, it appears in retrospect, is a man who has seen a vision of perfection: a man with a mission. That mission is to prepare us step by step to recognise ourselves, in the final book, as 'Yahoos in shape and disposition'. Only when we have read this final book do the mysterious elements in the book's opening letter become clear.

A LETTER FROM CAPTAIN GULLIVER TO COUSIN SYMPSON

An angry Gulliver complains about the faulty publication of his work, and laments, mysteriously, that he ever thought it worthwhile to attempt the reformation of 'the Yahoo race in this Kingdom'

In this opening letter, first added to the second edition, Captain Gulliver complains on Swift's behalf about changes made by the printer in the first edition, some real, and some imaginary. The fact that Swift sustains the fiction that the work is by Lemuel Gulliver is not the only joke. Throwing the reader in at the deep end, Swift sustains the characterisation of the Captain as he appears at the end of Part IV. Gulliver professes his inability to lie or to deceive, yet all the time he is referring solemnly to imaginary places and beings, and providing clues to Swift's satirical design. For instance, he names two of Swift's literary sources, first by claiming to be a cousin of Dampier, on whose

Voyage round the World the *Travels* are closely modelled, and later by rejecting the slanders that his work is fictional, or that it bears any relation to **Utopia**.

The letter is an excellent introduction to Swift's **ironic** method and to his use of the character of Gulliver. His most innocent disclaimers often turn out to be the most directly satirical strokes. For instance, disclaiming any lack of respect for Queen Anne, he thereby introduces her name and those of her ministers (Sidney Godolphin, Lord High Treasurer, and Robert Harley, Earl of Oxford) into the first page of the book. He professes not to understand the word 'innuendo', and then explicitly links 'people in power' to 'the Yahoos who are now said to govern the herd'. His list of the 'reformations' he expected his book to bring about is of course a summary of the criticisms of society made throughout the *Travels*. Yet he confesses to a conviction that Yahoos are not really 'capable of the least disposition to virtue or wisdom' and so are presumably incapable of reformation. He complains indignantly that readers have accused him of criticising statesmen, degrading human nature, and abusing the female sex – which is a pretty fair summary of what the book does throughout. So what are we to make of it all? Is Swift sending up his misanthropic sailor? Or distancing himself from the satirical content of his own work?

Dampier Sir William Dampier (1652–1715) published his vivid narrative of *A New Voyage round the World* in 1697

Utopia Sir Thomas More (1478–1535) published his *Utopia*, an account of an imaginary island with an ideal political system, in 1514

THE PUBLISHER TO THE READER

The publisher assures the reader that Lemuel Gulliver comes from respectable stock, and is a byword for truthfulness, if a little over-circumstantial

In his prefatory note the imaginary Richard Sympson offers a short and pedantic account of Lemuel Gulliver. He admits to 'some relation between us by the mother's side' without going so far as to say 'cousin

Gulliver'. Clearly this family of Gullivers and Sympsons is of a cautious disposition. Sympson claims to have removed from the text 'innumerable passages' of nautical pedantry to make the work more readable.

A VOYAGE TO LILLIPUT

CHAPTER 1   **Gulliver narrates his birth, education and career, up to his shipwreck and arrival in Lilliput**

By the fourth paragraph of a short autobiography, Gulliver has set sail from Bristol for a voyage to the South Seas. His ship, the *Antelope, is* wrecked on 5 November 1699 and Gulliver loses his companions when their lifeboat is overturned. He swims and wades ashore and, finding no inhabitants, falls asleep. When he wakes he finds that he cannot move: even his hair is tied to the ground. Something is creeping up his left leg, and when it reaches his chin he sees 'a human creature not six inches high'. Attempting to free himself, he is pierced by tiny arrows and decides not to resist. A 'person of quality' makes a long speech 'whereof I understood not one syllable', but he is fed on baskets of meat and barrels of wine. Feeling in debt to such hospitality, and drugged by wine, Gulliver relapses into sleep while the Lilliputians convey him ingeniously to their capital city. On arrival Gulliver is lodged in the nation's largest temple, into which he can just creep: secured by ninety-one watch-chains 'locked to my left leg with six and thirty padlocks'.

> Even in this chapter of eventful narrative, notice the play of Swift's **irony**. Gulliver has, on wakening, accepted his powerlessness in the hands of the Lilliputian state, and uses the most courteous titles in reference to his captors. What really chains him is his status as an Englishman with aspirations to gentility. He has begun also to note the language, and to observe the excellence of their science: so excellent, Gulliver claims, with unconscious irony, that they were able to raise him all of three inches in less than three hours. His own morality is also in question, however, as he contemplates treating his captors with no mercy on the grounds that they would be unable to resist.

The pride he takes in dividing the citizenry with a violent torrent of urine inaugurates a **theme** which is rarely silent in this work (and which critics of psychological and feminist critics find thematically revealing). In the very next chapter he will be inviting us to imagine how many Lilliputian wheelbarrows would be required to dispose of his morning stool. In Part II he falls into the stuff; in Part III he counsels inspecting the stools of politicians; in Part IV he himself is pelted with Yahoo excrements. Is Swift's 'excremental vision' a rebuke to human sentimentality and pride, or a pathological aspect of Swift himself?

Van Diemen's Land modern Tasmania

CHAPTER 2   **Gulliver begins ingratiating himself with his Imperial Majesty and his court, while an amusing inventory is made of the Man-Mountain's possessions**

Gulliver's delight in his new surroundings is reflected in Swift's entertaining description of events and objects. Yet Gulliver's pleasure in having his mercy to six ruffians well received at court, the corruption of Secretaries of State, who sell licences to people who wish to view the 'Man-Mountain', and the manner in which Gulliver is searched by security officers, whom he has to put in each pocket in turn, are none the less **satirical**, however solemn Gulliver's style of narration. An inventory of his possessions is made, in which common items, such as his snuff-box and comb, are described as they would be by somebody wholly ignorant of their purposes.

Many of these effects are already ironical, especially when Gulliver refers to the 'majestic' deportment of the Emperor, whom he has to observe by lying down, and who supposes that he can defend himself with his three-inch sword. Yet is there any reason why the 'deportment' of someone six inches high, and whom one later converses with while holding in one's hand, cannot be majestic? Would we be of less worth in any *moral* or *rational* characteristics if 1728 times smaller?

The inventory, in which we are required to guess the nature of everyday objects described through Lilliputian eyes, was the one passage singled out for praise by the illustrious critic Dr Samuel Johnson. It combines pleasure and surprise with the important effect of establishing the foreignness of Gulliver (it may take us some time to realise that Lilliput is in most political respects an **allegory** of England). The inventory also has a deeper satirical purpose. It suggests the similarly minute investigation made by the Whigs into the affairs of the fallen Tory leaders, Oxford and Bolingbroke, in 1715. Swift viewed Oxford especially as a giant among pygmies.

The Emperor with his 'Austrian lip', the Emperor is a satirical portrait of the Hanoverian King George I, who was anything but 'graceful' or 'well-proportioned' in unflattering eyes

High and Low Dutch German and Dutch

My pocket perspective pocket telescope

CHAPTER 3   **The entertainments of Lilliput described; and Gulliver's conditional liberty permitted**

An innocent opening paragraph leads directly into a chapter of court satire. Gulliver entertains and impresses the court himself, by assisting at military parades and exercises. He obtains his 'liberty' by consenting to a series of conditions devised by the Admiral of the Realm, beginning with an amusing form of address to the Emperor (not without some resemblance to styles of address used by some potentates today) and containing eight clauses. The seventh clause sentences Gulliver to hard labour in his leisure hours, and it is worth examining the other seven for their combination of prudence, oddity and sheer malignancy.

The practice of selecting candidates for high office by their skill in walking the tight-rope, or of awarding decorations to the most accomplished creepers, is clearly meant to typify the court of George I, or indeed any government. Blue, red and green ribbons signify the Orders of the Garter, the Bath and the Thistle. Gulliver seems impressed by his allowance of food sufficient for the support of 1728 Lilliputians (and by their ability to calculate 12 x 12 x 12 so minutely) but his reference to 'the prudent and exact economy of so great a prince' is not without irony, any more than his sense that he is now 'at full liberty'.

Flimnap the agile Flimnap is generally agreed to be a portrait of Sir Robert Walpole, and the 'cushion' which saves Flimnap's neck may be a reference to one of the king's mistresses, the Duchess of Kendal, who helped to restore Walpole to office in 1721. Walpole was first minister in 1715–17 and again from 1721 to 1742. For identification of other characters see Critical Approaches: Political Allegory

CHAPTER 4 The imperial metropolis is described and Gulliver finds a political situation remarkably suggestive of English Tories and Whigs at odds over relations between England and France

A description of the capital and the Emperor's palace is followed by an interview with Reldresal, Principal Secretary of Private Affairs (itself a satirical title), who outlines the political problems of the Empire. There are two factions, the High-Heels and Low-Heels. This division corresponds to the High and Low Church parties of Swift's day, the Tories and Whigs. George I favoured the latter but the Crown Prince kept in with both parties, that is, 'hobbled' with one heel higher than the other. A greater problem is that of the Big-Endian faction. The Big-Endians (who, like Catholics in England, were prevented from holding certain offices) are in league with the rival empire of Blefuscu, and Lilliput fears invasion by Blefuscu's new war fleet.

As a **satirist** Swift can depict the rivalry of factions with a keen sense of the ridiculous. As a politician and churchman he was in fact vigorous in promoting the interests of the Anglican Church against both Catholics and Dissenters. The author of *Gulliver's Travels* is a much more tolerant character than the Dean himself.

For fuller interpretation of this chapter see Historical Background and the discussion of Swift's political allegory in Critical Approaches. The 'bloody war' is the War of the Spanish Succession' (1701–13). 'His present Majesty's grandfather' is a loose reference to Henry VIII and the English Reformation. 'One Emperor lost his life, and another his crown': Charles I, executed in 1649, and James II, deposed in 1688

Those who wish to break their eggs from the big, not small, end.

=> v. effective satire

CHAPTER 5   **Gulliver captures Blefuscu's invasion fleet, and enrages His Majesty by refusing to subjugate Blefuscu absolutely; he puts out a fire in Her Majesty's apartment, but the tool Gulliver employs for the purpose incurs her abhorrence**

Gulliver wades across the channel between Lilliput and Blefuscu and captures fifty men-of-war which he tows back to Lilliput. For this feat he is created a Nardac (a Duke) but his reluctance to aid the Emperor in his plans to subjugate Blefuscu completely soon brings him into disfavour. A favourable treaty is arranged but his friendly relations with ambassadors from Blefuscu make matters still worse. In a second exploit Gulliver offends the Empress. He saves her palace from burning down by 'voiding' his urine 'in such a quantity ... that in three minutes the fire was wholly extinguished'.

> In one interpretation of the Palace fire incident, Gulliver represents Swift himself, the 'conflagration' suggests fires of religious enthusiasm, the 'noble pile, which had cost so many ages in erecting' is the Church of England, and the device by which the flames are extinguished is Swift's *A Tale of a Tub,* which so offended Queen Anne that Swift and his biographers regarded it as permanently barring his preferment. But the story also fits the Treaty of Utrecht, in which, by secret negotiations with the enemy, Oxford and Bolingbroke had used illegal means to extinguish a conflagration.

> Gulliver's disillusion with the Emperor's 'schemes' appears in his remark: 'Of so little weight are the greatest services to princes, when put into the balance with a refusal to gratify their passions' (p. 89). Is this consistent with his remark two paragraphs later that whispers against him at court led him to conceive for the first time 'some imperfect idea of Courts and Ministers'?

CHAPTER 6   **A chapter on laws, customs, education, social gatherings, and scandal-mongering**

After a playful comparison of the Lilliputian way of writing with that of ladies in England, Gulliver explains their burial rites, which he finds absurd, and passes on to other peculiar customs. These include punishing defrauders and false informers, rewarding merit, giving office to the virtuous rather than the intelligent, disqualifying atheists from office, executing the ungrateful, educating children in state nurseries (and allowing their parents to see them twice a year), and too many other points to list. Gulliver describes his social life and defends himself from the accusation of having had an affair with the Treasurer's wife, perhaps one of the least probable flirtations in imaginative literature.

This detailed account of Lilliputian customs and institutions is to be read warily. Although the nastiness of the Lilliputians is clear enough in Chapters 4 and 5, there is no guarantee that the same point of view will remain. Swift's attitude to the employment of atheists, or the education of working-class children, would not be that of a modern liberal, though he would certainly have liked begging to be 'a trade unknown in this kingdom'. Each point in this sometimes **Utopian** account of Lilliput should be weighed with care, and not just to detect what Swift might have thought, for he intends his reader to enjoy sifting the passage for its sense and nonsense, and Gulliver's **tone** makes it as hard as possible to distinguish between them. The passage constitutes a useful shortlist of some of Swift's presiding social themes.

Flimnap's white staff a white staff was the symbol of office of the English Lord Treasurer

CHAPTER 7   **Accused of high treason, the author escapes to Blefuscu**

Gulliver reveals how he was made aware of a plot to impeach him for treason. The articles of impeachment (in which Swift is satirising similar charges made against his friends) accuse him of 'maliciously' putting out a fire 'under colour of extinguishing' a fire, of conversing with ambassadors, whose business it is to converse, and treacherously planning a journey to Blefuscu with *only* his Imperial Majesty's permission. Parodying the arguments politicians (or people) can always find for the most despicable actions, Gulliver's informant explains how the court plans to take his life. First, he is to be blinded, as 'it would be sufficient for you to see by the eyes of the ministers, since the greatest princes do no more', then starved, by degrees, until his corpse is lean enough to cause the least threat to public health. But Gulliver takes advantage of 'his Imperial Majesty's licence' to visit Blefuscu, and having dutifully notified the Secretary, wades across the channel where he enjoys a reception 'suitable to the generosity of so great a prince'.

Gulliver's sceptical reference to the Emperor's 'lenity and tenderness' is one **ironical** note in his response, but you will detect others. Notice how Swift manages to suggest *both* that Gulliver's ludicrous sense of indebtedness might make him compliant, *and* that in reality the sentence was indeed a relatively mild one. Many political victims of our century might agree. Since the reference throughout is to the savage treatment of those involved in the Jacobite rising of 1715, and those alleged to have sympathised with it, the **allegory** makes a severe critique of state terror in England in 1715.

CHAPTER 8   **Finding an upturned boat, from the wreck of his own ship, Gulliver departs from Blefuscu, to the eventual relief of both Emperors, and returns home**

In Blefuscu Gulliver notices a 'real boat' off shore, and with the aid of twenty war-ships he beaches it. A demand arrives from Lilliput that Gulliver be sent back to them 'bound hand and foot'. The Emperor declares this to be impossible, and sends the good news of Gulliver's impending departure, while secretly asking our hero to remain in his service. He sets sail, recording his nautical progress as usual, and is soon picked up by an English merchant vessel, whose friendly captain finds Gulliver's story a little on the tall side. Six months later he arrives home, little changed by his experiences. He sets out again only two months later, having provided for his family.

However separate the conception of the four Parts, Swift utilises parallels between them as part of the ironic strategy. In Lilliput, Gulliver has generally seemed more human than his microscopic captors, as if moral worth and physical scale have some necessary connection: yet on leaving Lilliput he nonchalantly remarks that he had a mind to take home 'a dozen of the natives' as a souvenir, but that his Majesty engaged his honour not to do so, besides diligently searching his pockets. The irony at his Majesty's expense does not cancel out the ironising of Gulliver's moral relativity. In a further joke at Gulliver's expense Swift has him speculate on his plans to breed Lilliputian sheep for the wool trade, perhaps a foretaste of the Academy of Projectors in Part III.

The style of much of this final chapter reverts to the easy parody of nautical yarns, with a good salty tang to the descriptions, and a marvellous economy of narration. Underlying the surface narrative, however, the political allegory continues: Bolingbroke's exile in France (after the impeachment of himself and Oxford for alleged Jacobite sympathies) brought him into contact with the Pretender. Bolingbroke refused to flatter the Pretender's aspirations, so the latter was glad to see the back of him. This parallels somewhat Gulliver's realtionship with the Emperor, (see Historical and Literary Background).

A VOYAGE TO BROBDINGNAG

CHAPTER 1 — **After a disorienting voyage (the text talks of the Caspian sea and the Arctic, while the map shows a peninsula off California, then Drake's 'Nova Albion') Gulliver is abandoned in a land of Giants and adopted by a farmer's family**

[handwritten margin note: role reversed from Part I – i.e. it is Gulliver who is the tiny one now]

With Captain Nicholas of Cornwall, Gulliver sets sail for Surat in the *Adventure*. After wintering at the Cape of Good Hope they run into foul weather and are blown five hundred leagues off course. Ashore in search of water, Gulliver is abandoned by his shipmates who are chased off by a 'monster'. He finds himself in a cornfield being harvested by people as tall as church steeples. Taken home by a farmer he describes his first experience of life in a giant family, with baby, cat, dogs and rats all of terrifying proportions. He is almost swallowed by a year-old child, and is horrified at the sight of the baby feeding from a 'monstrous' nipple. As in the first chapter of Part I, Gulliver gives a circumstantial account of his first experience of discharging 'the necessities of nature'.

Gulliver in this opening chapter seems like, yet unlike, the **narrator** of Part I. For instance, 'knowing' that human creatures are more savage and cruel in proportion to their 'bulk' he expects to be eaten by these 'barbarians'. In this respect Gulliver seems blessed with a very short memory; yet in other ways he is the same toadying Englishman. When his finder treats him as one would 'a small dangerous animal' (the size **theme** again) Gulliver ingratiates himself with his captors by a display of humility and good manners.

Mathematicians will grasp how much less of a problem 'the necessities of nature' would present than they did in Lilliput, yet, if anything, Gulliver's embarrassment is increased. Critics have never quite known how to handle Swift's fascination with excreta; is he exhibiting an unhealthy obsession, or diagnosing something fundamental to the human psyche? Is the monstrous breast and sceptical reference to English complexions a sign of misogyny, or simply the obverse of his own monstrousness and monstrous odours in Lilliput? Physicality is clearly going to be a major theme of this book. Anal and genital gratifications loom large.

CHAPTER 2   **Of Glumdalclitch, her little Grildrig, and their journey of three thousand miles to Lorbrulgrud**

Gulliver is adopted by Glumdalclitch, the nine-year-old daughter of the house. She calls him 'Grildrig' or mannikin. News of his arrival spreads, and Gulliver's 'master', as he already calls him, decides to make a quick fortune by exhibiting this entertaining freak. He is carried about in a box and shown at the nearest market town with such success that they set out on a two-month tour of towns and country houses on the way to the capital, Lorbrulgrud, or 'Pride of the Universe'. Glumdalclitch teaches him the language.

Gulliver's rapid adaptation to his new scale is shown in the humour of his reference to Glumdalclitch as his little nurse, 'not above forty foot high, being little for her age'. Sometimes Gulliver seems disoriented: in the previous chapter he refers, oddly, to regarding his master 'from the height of fifty foot'; in this he becomes infantile, a doll, consenting to be dressed and undressed by the nine-year-old Glumdalclitch; in the next he will be disgusted by the Queen crunching immense poultry bones between her teeth, forgetful that he himself devoured whole oxen in Lilliput.

[handwritten margin note: passive but at times more active, his opinions if not actions*]*

CHAPTER 3   The proud author is 'sent for to Court', disputes with great scholars, is in high favour with the Queen, but quarrels with her dwarf

Frequent exhibitions damage Gulliver's health, but after an appearance at court he is bought by the Queen who also takes Glumdalclitch into her service. The King at first takes him for a 'splacknuck', as does everyone else (Gulliver has already assured us that a splacknuck, though a small animal, is 'very finely shaped'). Next he is taken for a clockwork toy. The court scholars, like those of Lilliput, do not really believe in his existence and finally pronounce him a *lusus naturae* (Latin for a freak of nature). A cabinet-maker produces a wooden house for him, 'like a London bed-chamber' says Gulliver, though resembling a doll's-house. He dines with the Queen, another nauseous experience, and talks with the king about 'the manners, religion, laws, government and learning of Europe' to the great merriment of the king who 'observed how contemptible a thing was human grandeur, which could be mimicked by such diminutive insects as I'.

> While Gulliver writhes in embarrassment at his failure to impress the king, Swift puts into the king's mouth his own views of human society which is now seen clearly as Lilliputian. Gulliver also begins to see something of his own absurdity, at least physically, as he suffers indignities at the hands of the Queen's dwarf and fights off flies and wasps the size of larks and partridges. At a deeper level the chapter is concerned with the limitations of reason, the ease with which his Majesty's great scholars deceive themselves by false reasoning (pp. 142–3) and the pretensions of science and philosophy to certain knowledge.
>
> **The Royal Sovereign** a large British warship built in 1637
> **Gresham College** a science institute which housed the Royal Society until 1666

CHAPTER 4   Of the pleasures, horrors and disappointments of the traveller

The country is described. Although the size of North America it does not appear on any maps, and it has no ports: since whales are the only seafood large enough to eat there is no fishing industry. The account of the capital is notable for Gulliver's description of its beggars with their cancers and lice. A travelling closet is made for Gulliver, but he is not an impressionable tourist. Travelling in a coach the size of Westminster Hall, Gulliver is disappointed by the tower of the nation's chief temple: 'the height is not above three thousand foot'. For some reason he is more impressed by finding a 'little finger' four feet long, fallen from a statue, and by the king's oven, though it is 'not so wide ... as the cupola of St Paul's'.

It is only natural that Gulliver should be most interested in things whose size is within his grasp: and Swift is concerned with the horror of human realities more than with the grandeur of human impossibilities. A **feminist critic** has seen Gulliver's reference to a beggar woman's cancerous breast, with holes into which 'I could have crept' as a macabre and misogynist sexual fantasy. Might one take it otherwise? In another detail, the humour of a being as tiny as Gulliver expressing disdain for something only three thousand feet tall may hint at Swift's awareness of theories of sublimity, in which the mind itself enlarges in response to massive stimuli (Burke's *Philosophical Enquiry* into these matters was not published until 1757 but the ideas in it were debated much earlier).

St Paul's the City of London's famous cathedral, designed by Sir Christopher Wren (1632–1723), was finished in 1716, replacing an earlier cathedral which had been severely damaged in the Great Fire of London, 1666. The central dome reaches 365 feet

CHAPTER 5   **Gulliver is at risk from hailstones, mole-holes, Maids of Honour, frogs and monkeys**

The dwarf repays a foolish pun by showering Gulliver with apples the size of barrels, and Gulliver suffers other calamities. He is picked up by a spaniel, falls into a mole-hill, does battle with a linnet and jumps into a fresh heap of cow-dung. Hit by hailstones he finds it necessary to 'weigh and measure' them in order to discover that they are 'near eighteen hundred times as large as those in Europe' (is this a comment on Gulliver's pedantry, or that of scientists in general?). But three episodes in the chapter are of deeper significance. He is used as a sexual toy by the people punish Gulliver like pet (eg end of chapter five)

Queen's Maids of Honour. After this erotic (?) interlude Swift cuts directly to a scene of execution, which is robbed of none of its force by Gulliver's calm description. But the longest episode in the chapter shows Gulliver kidnapped by a monkey who attempts to suckle him like an infant. Gulliver's attempts to regain his, and our, dignity, are greeted with mockery by the Court.

That the monkey is the only creature in Brobdingnag who really regards Gulliver as one of his own species is one of Swift's most calculated shocks to the complacency of his reader (remember that Darwin's *The Descent of Man* was not published until 1871). It also prepares for the manner in which Gulliver is brought to recognise his kinship with the Yahoos in Part IV: nursing and copulation are among the most species-specific activities, and may constitute scientific proof of membership of the same species.

Gulliver's experiences in the hands and bosoms of the Maids of Honour allow Swift one of his most wicked assaults on court morals. While he is accusing them of sexual licence, and indulging in a little sexual fantasy, he slips in a calculated insult on the subject of smell: 'I cannot forbear doing justice to the Queen … and Glumdalclitch, whose persons were as sweet as those of any lady in England', who, by implication smell eighteen hundred times worse than they ought. Is this misogyny, or **realism** about eighteenth-century hygiene, when washing or changing clothes was an unusual event?

CHAPTER 6   **Gulliver attempts to impress the king by playing a gigantic baby harpsichord, missing half the notes, and by discoursing on the English Constitution, with similar omissions**

Gulliver amuses himself making a comb out of hairs from the king's beard, and attempting to play the spinet (a small harpsichord), but this amusing opening is the prelude to Swift's sharpest **satire** in the second voyage. Wishing for 'the tongue of Demosthenes or Cicero' (the greatest orators of Greece and Rome respectively) Gulliver attempts to impress the king with a description of his 'own dear native country'. He does this very eloquently, in terms very far from those Swift would use, but the

pg 128

king proposes a number of innocent but searching questions, to each of which it would be hard to give an answer at once honest and encouraging. In the final paragraph, after a careful review of all the evidence, the king delivers to 'my little friend Grildrig' a devastating judgement: 'I cannot but conclude the bulk of your natives, to be the most pernicious race of little odious vermin that Nature ever suffered to crawl upon the surface of the earth'.

The **ironic** and rhetorical arrangement of this whole chapter is worth the closest study, with its slow and logical build-up, the deceptively amicable setting, and the measured and unanswerable final sentence. The king is clearly an expert cross-examiner, or rather Swift is adept at mounting a satirical attack by nothing more than a series of rhetorical questions, of which those on the law (p. 170) are among the best examples. (The corruption of lawyers is an obsessive **theme** of the work and returns forcefully in Part IV). Of course Gulliver's speech, with its inflated praise for illustrious and valorous peers, saintly and learned bishops, wise and freely elected MPs, etc., is ironical in itself. The gentleness of the king's cross-examination merely sharpens the attack. The last sentence should be learned by heart (and, perhaps, taken to heart?).

Demosthenes a great Athenian orator, Demosthenes (c.383–322BC) was a noble but somewhat humourless character. A master of words and argument, he rarely flattered his audience

Cicero Marcus Tullius Cicero (106–43BC) was consul of Rome in 63BC. Murdered by the second triumvirate, Antony, Octavian and Lepidus, after the assassination of Caesar, he was an unbending idealist who developed a clear and fluent style in his many writings on law, government and moral philosophy

generals richer than our Kings a biting reference to the Duke of Marlborough, enriched by years of soldiering

CHAPTER 7   **On gunpowder, the practical arts, good government, and the Glorious Revolution**

The attack on human folly, duplicity and depravity is now sustained without relief, but by a variety of means. First, Gulliver confesses that the king's verdict is based on partial evidence, for 'I artfully eluded many of his questions'. Then, he attempts to explain the king's reaction as the effect of 'a certain narrowness of thinking' (literally narrow as opposed to broad, but by implication narrow as opposed to lax?). And next he attempts to please the king by offering him the secret of gunpowder, which he commends by a catalogue of the ways which civilised nations have devised to destroy as many of each other as possible. But this king is a poor political philosopher, ignorant of 'mystery, refinement, and intrigue' and has no desire to exterminate his people. In the remainder of the chapter the **Utopian** element of Brobdingnag becomes apparent. It is a land of useful science, simple laws, and good agriculture. Apart from a work of moral philosophy which looks back to an age when men must have been much larger, since they are now so physically frail, their books are few and profound. Gulliver approves of their prose style, in a verdict on Swift's own.

> From the opening section, in which Gulliver acts like a minuscule arms trader, to the close, this chapter addresses the vital importance of maintaining the ideal constitutional balance established by the 'Glorious Revolution' of 1688. At the close, Gulliver wonders why Brobdingnag needs an army at all. He is told that even in Brobdingnag there used to be wars, 'the nobility often contending for power, the people for liberty, and the king for absolute dominion', but that two reigns ago a 'general composition' was agreed by all three parties (a reference to the ideal balance established by the Glorious Revolution) since when the 'militia' have been kept under firm restrictions. Brobdingnag has solved the perennial constitutional problem of a balanced constitution, and replaced a standing army by a well-trained voluntary militia. One of the things that makes Swift's core political beliefs, as opposed to his day-to-day political alignments, very hard to place is that both Tories of the so-called 'country party' and radical republicans shared a hostility towards standing armies.
>
> **General composition** clearly represents the Revolution Settlement which was the basis of Swift's political views. But Brobdingnag has evidently learned how to do without standing armies; England, Swift implies, has not

*construction of idea that Gulliver is a pet Gullivers
 - King wishes to find a female from the Gulliver
   race to use breed more small people
SUMMARIES   A VOYAGE TO LAPUTA, BALNIBARBI, ...

 - pedigree pet but pet all the same

CHAPTER 8   Dropped in the ocean by an eagle, Gulliver returns to
             normality and has a hard time getting adjusted

The King begins to think of breeding more creatures like Gulliver (he is
clearly beginning to be corrupted, as Gulliver was in Lilliput) but the
latter is returned to liberty by the aid of a passing eagle who flies off with
his box and drops it into the sea. Still inside his box Gulliver wonders
why the captain of a passing ship does not order one of his sailors to 'put
his finger into the ring' and lift the box on board. His rescuer, Captain
Willcocks of Shropshire, treats Gulliver kindly, but is troubled by his
apparent insanity until the whole story has been told, and some of
Gulliver's remarkable souvenirs produced in evidence.

The size of everything on the ship provokes Gulliver to laughter,
and he explains that he had accustomed himself to life in
Brobdingnag where 'I winked at my own littleness as people do at   145
their own faults': one of numerous passages in which Swift
comments obliquely on the moral reference of his games with scale.
Nine months later he has still not come to terms with his real
stature, as his comical homecoming shows. Is this also a comment
on the ease of getting things out of perspective?

Places Among the place-names in this chapter, Tonquin is Tongking,
Vietnam; New Holland is Australia

A VOYAGE TO LAPUTA, BALNIBARBI, GLUBBDUBDRIB,
  LUGGNAGG, AND JAPAN

CHAPTER 1   Taken by pirates, and betrayed by a Dutchman, the
             author on his third voyage is rescued from a desert
             island by a flying one

Gulliver is persuaded by Captain William Robinson to be surgeon on the
Hope-well for a voyage to the East Indies, and they set sail in August
1706 via Fort St George (Madras). To pass the time during delays at
Tonquin, Gulliver takes command of a sloop – a small single-masted
vessel – which is first caught in a storm and then boarded by pirates, who
include a Japanese captain and a Dutch sailor. Gulliver's men are taken
prisoner, while he himself is 'set adrift in a small canoe' thanks to the

153/ speaks to Islanders in Italian — hoping "the cadence might be more agreeable to his ears" — v. clever Gulliver, is accepted (to an extent) by after of chair to lift him

A VOYAGE TO LAPUTA, BALNIBARBI, ...   SUMMARIES

CHAPTER 1 continued

Japanese who obstructs the Dutchman's more hostile intentions. He makes his way to some distant islands which appear uninhabited. Walking in the heat of the day he is surprised to find the sun suddenly obscured by a flying island. He attracts the attention of these airborne islanders, first by shouting and then with his habitual 'supplicating postures', and is lifted into the island.

> The inclusion of Japan with four wholly fantastical countries seems to hint at the magical status of Japan, which was at that time still closed to all but the most persistent and favoured foreigners, while suspending disbelief in the others. Foreign trade with Japan was monopolised throughout the sixteenth to eighteenth centuries first by Portugal and then by Holland, with occasional English intrusions. Whichever nation was in favour at the time did its best to exclude the others; hence the conduct of the Dutch sailor in this chapter, and Gulliver's behaviour in Chapter 11. This chapter is one of numerous points where the imperial conduct of 'the West', and the exportation of Western conflicts, is subjected to unusually exact scrutiny.

CHAPTER 2   **An account of the strange practices of these absent-minded, hyper-intellectual, transcendental aerialists, their flappers, and their very frustrated women**

Swift's **satire** on intellectual absurdities opens with a description of the islanders. The people of 'quality', that is, the ruling class, are perpetually lost in deep speculation, their heads inclined to left or right, 'one of their eyes turned inward, and the other directly up to the zenith'. Their clothes are decorated with (and their food cut into) astronomical and musical figures. 'Flappers' remind their absent-minded masters that they were about to speak, or are being spoken to, or are in danger of collision, by gently flapping their mouth, ears or eyes, with a bladder full of dried peas. Gulliver gives the court 'a very mean opinion of my understanding' by refusing the aid of a flapper. Clothes don't fit, and houses are ill-built for the same reason: his hosts, being interested only in theoretical mathematics, despise practical geometry. Nature has adapted their ears to 'hear the music of the spheres' but they never enjoy 'a minute's peace of mind', living in perpetual dread of the earth's destruction by a comet, or of its falling into the sun, or of the sun's losing its energy (all actual fears of contemporary astronomers). Hence the 'common pleasures' of life are denied to them, and their neglected wives long to escape to the 'diversions of the metropolis', as one court lady succeeded in doing, to 'live in rags, having pawned her clothes to maintain an old deformed footman, who beat her every day'.

16 O (handwritten)

Gulliver puts this down to 'the caprices of womankind', but Swift, having noted that the Laputans are strangers to 'imagination, fancy and invention', seems on this occasion to find such behaviour very understandable. It is significant that in this third book, with its satire on intellectual deformities, normal human behaviour – which Swift disapproves of elsewhere – is often used as his satiric standard. — *here "normal" = "reasonable"* (handwritten)

behaviour ridiculous but somewhat admirable (handwritten marginal note)

Here, learning the local language requires a special investment in astronomical, geometrical and musical terms, while Swift slips in a parody of improbable etymology in Gulliver's speculation on the origin of the word 'Laputa', probably to invite the reader to catch the echo of *La puta* (Spanish for whore) and consider what is being prostituted. Intelligence? Science? Uses and abuses of language will be a major **theme** of this Part. And 'prostitute writers' are a butt of Chapter 8.

CHAPTER 3   **In a parody of the language of scientific treatises Gulliver explains magnetic suspension, and its political applications**

Gulliver gives an elaborate technical account of the island's magnetic system of suspension and propulsion, and relates its inhabitants' astronomical discoveries. His account of the political relations between Laputa and the land of Balnibarbi beneath it is more pointed. It describes the methods by which the king can reduce his subjects to obedience, either by depriving them of sun and rain and so 'afflict the inhabitants with death and diseases', or by letting the island drop on their heads. The cities can, however, defend themselves from this fate either by sheltering under natural rocks or by erecting artificial towers strong enough to shatter the bottom of the island. This 'balance of advantage' by which the inhabitants are able to protect 'their liberty or property' was once applied ingeniously by the rebellious people of Lindalino who used magnetic powers of their own to counter those of the island.

government and rebellion,

thin line between suppression of a people and their destruction.

Whether we interpret the island as monarchy, or as government, or as the colonial power of England, in which case Lindalino's 'proud people' are the people of Dublin, it is clear that all Gulliver's pseudo-science about loadstones and adamant is a Swiftian **allegory** about the relations between governors and governed. It has a remarkably republican tinge. The last five paragraphs allegorise Ireland's campaign against 'Wood's half-pence', an unpopular currency imposed on Ireland. In this allegory Swift's own Drapier's Letters are no doubt the 'combustible fuel' which helps to repel Laputa.

CHAPTER 4   **Tired of abstractions, Gulliver descends to Balnibarbi, witnessing the devastation caused by Laputan-inspired projectors**

Through the friendship of a 'great lord at court' Gulliver obtains permission to descend to Balnibarbi, where he stays with Lord Munodi. He finds the people 'generally in rags' and despite signs of labour 'I never knew a soil so unhappily cultivated, houses so ill-contrived and so ruinous, or a people whose countenances and habit expressed so much misery and want'. Munodi himself has an estate which is neat, ordered, and productive, and a noble house 'built according to the best rules of ancient architecture'. But he is generally despised and mistrusted 'for managing his affairs no better' and will soon have to conform to 'modern usage' as devised by the Academy of Projectors.

It would be complacent to think that this chapter is wholly about eighteenth-century Ireland, but Gulliver's shock recalls Swift's anger over the Irish poor, who starved while economic 'projectors' wrangled over schemes of reform, of which his own *Modest Proposal* is in part a savage parody. While the Academy devises new rules for all trades and activities, 'the whole country lies miserably waste, the houses in ruins, and the people without food or clothes'.

Lord Munodi 'Munodi' partly represents Oxford again, but Swift himself also put much energy into maintaining his house and land in model order

CHAPTER 5 A description of the grand Academy of Lagado and its professors' attempts to improve on the useful arts by theory-driven experiments

A chapter of sheer high spirits in which Gulliver soberly reports on the projects of the Academy for 'extracting sunbeams out of cucumbers', 'softening marble for pillows and pin-cushions', reforming language by abolishing words and many other hilarious attempts to reverse the natural order.

Some readers cite this chapter as proof of Swift's anti-intellectualism. He certainly based some of his 'projects' on actual scientific proceedings at the Royal Society.

CHAPTER 6 A visit to the school of political projectors

i.e. what would appear to the reader (one today) as being wholly reasonable and expected

The professors in the 'school of political projectors' appear to be 'wholly out of their senses', indulging in 'wild and impossible schemes'. The first project allows Swift to express his opinion of the mental health of senators by an ingenious list of their bodily ills, after which Gulliver offers advice on memorable ways of reminding ministers of their duty. A scheme for ending political factions by brain surgery shows how **ironical** Swift can be about his own fierce party loyalties.

The opening paragraph is an example of Swift's technique of 'reversal' at its best and it would be unforgivable to explain what happens to the reader who still thinks he can trust Gulliver as a guide. This chapter of hard-hitting political **satire** concludes with a direct attack on the methods of investigation used in 'the kingdom of Tribnia, by the natives called Langden', where unscrupulous ministers pervert the most innocent letters into proofs of treason. Swift's list of examples is far from innocent. Tribnia and Langden are of course **anagrams** for Britain and England: Swift is taking his revenge on those who used such evidence against his friends. In a flight of **invective** he gaily calls Walpole a 'buzzard' and his administration 'a running sore'.

CHAPTER 7   An excursion to Glubbdubdrib, the Island of Sorcerers
or Magicians

Gulliver sails from Maldonada to Glubbdubdrib, whose governor has the
power of calling up the dead to serve him for twenty-four hours, which
may be why the palace guards make Gulliver's 'flesh creep with a horror
I cannot express'. Of the many heroes of antiquity whom Gulliver is
enabled to meet, Brutus is described with the most wholehearted
admiration – apparently shared by Caesar. 'I had the honour to
have much conversation with Brutus; and was told that his ancestor
Junius, Socrates, Epaminondas, Cato the younger, Sir Thomas More and
himself, were perpetually together'.

> When Gulliver comments that Brutus and the five other ancients
> were 'a sextumvirate to which all the ages of the world cannot
> add a seventh' he is expressing Swift's own preference for the
> ancients over the moderns (as in Swift's *Battle of the Books*). The
> implied admiration for the stoic values of this sextumvirate may
> also be a reading instruction: understanding what these six men
> stood for will help you to decide which parts of the *Travels*
> most nearly express Swift's true beliefs, and whether Lilliput,
> Brobdingnag or the stoic realm of Houyhnhnmland is nearest to his
> own **Utopia**
>
> Gulliver sees many other characters, especially 'destroyers of
> tyrants', and 'restorers of liberty to oppressed and injured nations',
> but in a satirical insult to the reader, he clearly does not think that
> we would be much interested in these.

Alexander Alexander the Great (356–23BC) expanded Greek power
throughout the Mediterranean lands and into Asia. In the battle of Arbela
(near the river Tigris) he defeated King Darius III of Persia to win control of
Babylon and Persepolis. He died of fever, but there was a legend that he
was poisoned

Hannibal this great Governor of Carthage (c.247–183BC) led an army of
60,000 across the Alps to attack Rome from the North, in a campaign that
lasted fifteen years. The Roman poet Livy suggested that Hannibal used
vinegar to soften an Alpine rock-fall

The sextumvirate:
Lucius Junius Brutus was first Consul of Rome in 509BC, after expelling the Tarquin rulers. He executed his own sons for treason
Marcus Brutus (85–42BC) took his own life when he failed to prevent the restoration of tyranny after he had assassinated Caesar
Marcus Porcius Cato (95–46BC) the embodiment of stoic Roman virtues, helped his friends to escape a siege but took his own life rather than submit to tyranny
Socrates (c.470–399BC) was sentenced to death for impiety, but refused to change his opinions
Epaminondas (420–362BC) military commander of Thebes, was also relentlessly truthful. He lived hardily and died a heroic death in battle
Sir Thomas More (1475–1535) executed by Henry VIII for 'treason', was subsequently canonised

CHAPTER 8   **Further dialogue with the Ancients convinces Gulliver that modern writers have prostituted their art, and modern politicians have prostituted inherited virtues**

Next Gulliver calls up Homer and Aristotle, with all their critics and interpreters who appear ashamed at having 'so horribly misrepresented the meaning of those authors to posterity'. With this warning to Swift's critics, including us, Gulliver introduces the poet and philosopher to two of their commentators. Swift makes Aristotle guilty of a punning reference to Duns Scotus by asking 'whether the rest of the tribe were as great dunces'. Descartes is summoned to explain his system of philosophy to Aristotle who expresses Swift's view of all modern theories, such as Newtonian gravity ('attraction'), as merely 'new fashions'. Inspecting the ancestry of certain noble families, Gulliver finds their lineages interrupted by 'pages, lackeys, valets' and the like. From this scurrilous enquiry he passes to a detailed examination of modern history and discovers 'the true causes of many great events that have surprised the world, how a whore can govern the back-stairs, the back-stairs a council, and the council a senate'.   —   *idea of whore return)*

Swift's attack on the illusion of progress is at its most rigorous when suggesting that Aristotle was more modest and less deluded than

Descartes or Newton. Is the frivolous attitude to Newton one of his less impressive characteristics?

The attack on lineage cannot be summarised. Swift's unrelenting attack on every kind of treachery, vice and injustice is clearly intended to describe the normal state of affairs, not the exception. Few passages in the book are as bleak as this, though the discovery of 'a barber, an abbot, and two cardinals' in one royal line is typical of many comic touches. To an insider such as Swift it was a simple fact that the Stuart kings, Charles II and James II especially, were governed by their mistresses. Great titles were bestowed on sexual favourites, and cases of doubtful parentage were frequent in some great families of the day. Again, rather curiously for the Tory Swift, the final paragraph seems to yearn for a yeoman, and perhaps republican, 'spirit of liberty'.

Homer (dates unknown, probably about the ninth century BC) Greek poet of *The Iliad* and *The Odyssey*. The earliest and most influential of all known poets. He was traditionally thought to be blind in old age, but Gulliver remarks on his 'quick and piercing eyes'

Aristotle (384–22BC) the great philosopher and scientist who enrolled in Plato's academy when he was seventeen and whose most famous works – *The Physics, The Metaphysics, The Ethics, The Poetics, The Rhetoric, The Politics* – dominated studies in these subjects for nearly two thousand years

Didymus (born 63BC in Alexandria) lived in Rome and wrote a treatise on Homer

Eustathius Archbishop of Thessalonica in the twelfth century, commentator on Homer

Ramus Petrus Ramus, or Pierre de la Ramu (1515–72), was a leading opponent of Aristotle's ideas in the sixteenth century

Scotus Duns Scotus (*c.*1270–1308) wrote chiefly about Aquinas and Aristotle

Descartes Rene Descartes (1596–1650), philosopher, physicist and mathematician, questioned Aristotle's physics. His theory of vortices attempted to explain the movements of the planets

Gassendi Pierre Gassendi (1592–1655) criticised both Aristotle and Descartes

Newton Sir Isaac Newton (1642–1727) made revolutionary discoveries in mathematics, optics, and astronomy. He was the co-developer of integral and differential calculus, which he called 'fluxions'; he analysed light, using prisms; and his greatest work, the *Principia*, described the mechanics of the solar system. He calculated the gravitational pull of the earth on the moon, and went on to describe the law of universal gravitation

Eliogabalus a particularly cruel Emperor of Rome, who reigned from AD 218 to 222, when he was assassinated at the age of eighteen

Agesilaus King of Sparta, 397–60BC

Polydore Virgil an Italian who lived in England and in 1534 published his *History of England*

'Nec vir fortis, nec fæmina casta' (Latin) neither one brave man nor one chaste woman

Actium Octavius Caesar defeated Antony and Cleopatra at this battle in 31BC

CHAPTER 9   **Gulliver licks the dust before the footstool of the despotic King of Luggnagg who, luckily, delights in his company**

seems to abandon the near-Republican spirit he expressed in the previous chapter

Gulliver sails to Luggnagg, where he receives royal permission to visit the king and 'to lick the dust before his footstool', a literal invitation which ensures that petitioners have their mouths too full of dust to speak by the time they reach the throne, and also provides a convenient way of poisoning the king's enemies. As his destination is Japan, Gulliver is now travelling as 'a Dutchman'.

Gulliver's republican spirit seems to desert him in his response to this monarch; but Swift's sense of humour is wonderfully shown in the language of Luggnagg (try saying the sentence at the top of page 251: does your mouth seem full of dust?).

CHAPTER 10   **Gulliver is cured of the desire for immortality**

Hearing of a race of immortals known as Struldbruggs, Gulliver amuses his hosts by expressing 'rapture' at this discovery, but his rapture soon turns to horror. The Struldbruggs are not the models of virtue and wisdom he imagines, but 'the most mortifying sight I ever beheld', having 'not only all the follies and infirmities of other old men, but many more which arose from the dreadful prospect of never dying'.

This parable has several meanings. It can be read as a sermon, such as Swift might have preached to help people conquer 'the fear of death', or perhaps as a **satire** on the way people blame their shortcomings on the shortness of life. It is also a joke at Gulliver's expense. Compare the final sentence of the chapter, for instance ('avarice is the necessary consequent of old age'), with Gulliver's description at the start of what he would do first if he 'were sure to live for ever'.

At the start of the next chapter Gulliver assures his readers that this story is unlike anything he has seen 'in any book of travels', which is Swift's exceedingly backhanded way of acknowledging that he got the idea from the well-known classical legend of Tithonus (a prince of Troy who was also granted immortality but denied eternal youth).

CHAPTER 11   **Gulliver visits Tokyo and Nagasaki and Swift delivers a gratuitous insult to Dutch Protestants**

Gulliver takes a ship to Japan and is received by the Emperor (one of the least probable events in the book, but Gulliver tells us nothing about it) who agrees to send him to Nangasac (modern Nagasaki). There he joins a Dutch ship and sails home via Amsterdam.

To understand the 'business of the Crucifix' one must remember that Nagasaki was the site of a mass martyrdom of Christians who had been converted by Portuguese Jesuits. The Dutch were careful to dissociate themselves from the religion of their rivals. As Swift disapproved of the extent of Dutch religious tolerance he represents them as literally 'trampling on the Crucifix' in the interests of commerce. His attitude to the republican Dutch is one indication of a fundamental Toryism in his political ideals.

the *Amboyna* this Dutch ship bears the name of a port in the East Indies where a massacre of the English occurred in 1623

CHAPTER 1   **Captain Gulliver's first command ends in mutiny and he finds himself in a strange land whose humanoid creatures he describes as animals**

After five months at home Gulliver sails via the West Indies to the South Seas, as Captain of the *Adventure*. His crew mutiny, confine him to cabin and then set him ashore in a strange land. He explores stealthily, expecting to be set upon by savages, and comes across 'several animals'. He is approached by one of these beasts in human shape and hits it with the flat of his sword, attracting a crowd of others who pelt him with excrement. Gulliver is saved by the arrival of a horse 'who' inspects him carefully and then consults another horse. They are both perplexed and use 'various gestures, not unlike those of a philosopher, when he would attempt to solve some new and difficult phenomenon'. Gulliver decides they must be magicians in disguise and 'Upon the strength of this reasoning' makes a polite speech. He learns two words, 'Yahoo' and 'Houyhnhnm', and practises saying them with the right accent.

> The opening account of Gulliver's command is full of intriguing clues to his state of mind even before his crew mutinies. If one sees Gulliver as a character and the *Travels* as a novel, it is possible to feel that this calamity has disturbed the balance of mind. One's reading of Part IV depends very much on how much importance one attaches to this. The first creatures he meets sound remarkably human from his description, yet he comments 'Upon the whole, I never beheld in all my travels so disagreeable an animal, nor one against which I naturally conceived so strong an antipathy': their faces are ignored, but he seems fascinated by their pudenda. Meeting next with what are clearly horses, he addresses them as gentlemen, and with his usual obsequiousness to persons of quality. Note how the Yahoo greets him almost exactly as Gulliver greets the Houyhnhnm, but Gulliver's response is violent, the horse's polite. Has Gulliver become a misanthrope? Or has he really met superior beings in horses' shape?

Yahoo 'Yahoo' has entered the English language as a term of abuse for people who behave contemptibly. Spoken 'in a loud voice, imitating ... the neighing of a horse' it sounds half-way between a contemptuous snort and various derisory expressions like 'Yah!'. English Yahoos in many districts call each other's attention by shouting 'Yoo-hoo'

Houyhnhnm 'Houyhnhnm' may be said in two syllables as whin-im (like whinny) or in four, who-on-'n-im (like the four or five distinct syllables in a longer neigh)

CHAPTER 2   **Gulliver is received into a Houyhnhnm household**

presumes them to have masters due to their appearance

Still expecting to meet the human masters of these horses, Gulliver is led to a spacious stable, where he is further surprised to see horses engaged in various domestic activities. He is introduced by the gray horse to a 'very comely mare' with her colt and foal, after which they put him next to a Yahoo for purposes of comparison. Unable to eat either Yahoo-food or the horses' oats he is given a bowl of milk. 'An old steed, who seemed to be of quality' arrives in a sledge drawn by four Yahoos, to dine with the family. After making himself some porridge, Gulliver is found a place to sleep, between the house of the Houyhnhnms and the stable of the Yahoos. ⟶ *is neither one nor the other*

v. different - horse driven by Yahoos!

In this chapter Gulliver is horrified to recognise 'in this abominable animal, a perfect human figure' and he is relieved that his clothing partly disguises this resemblance from the horses. Is man a clothed Yahoo? Several definitions of human superiority are explored throughout this book: that of man as toolmaker comes to mind when we note Gulliver's evasiveness concerning who makes the mats, or builds the stables, or indeed milks the cows, or why the Houyhnhnms have not invented the wheel.

CHAPTER 3   **Gulliver's host teaches him the language, and discovers the secret of his clothing**

humans - at a base level - are like Yahoos), Aim to be like the Houghnhnm but are

He sets about learning the language, which is nasal and guttural, 'like High Dutch or German ... but more graceful and significant'. His master, astonished to find a Yahoo so teachable, is eager to learn how he came by his 'appearance of reason'. Every explanation Gulliver makes to his master tends to confirm the **theme** that men are Yahoos who have learned to 'imitate a rational creature'. Even to account for his arrival Gulliver has to explain to his noble master the meanings of mutiny and desertion! The horse is unable to believe that Yahoos could build a boat of any kind, but as he has no conception of lying or falsehood he can only accuse Gulliver, in a phrase the Greek philosopher Plato might have used, of 'saying the thing which was not'. The Houyhnhnm finally detects that but for the 'false covering' with which he hides his real nature, and his 'affectation' of walking on his hind legs, Gulliver would be a perfect Yahoo.

> Just how seriously are we to take this Part? Our own claims to 'Reason' are under scrutiny throughout the *Travels*, but is it rational to teach language to a creature with only the appearance of reason? The Houyhnhnms are as dogmatic as the scholars of Brobdingnag, for Gulliver's master *knew* 'it was impossible that there could be a country beyond the sea'. Are the Horses really rational beings, or only, in their own phrase, 'the Perfection of Nature'? Is it significant that Gulliver vacillates between recognising his kinship with the Yahoos and regarding them as raw materials for making clothes, or covering for his boat?

Houyhnhnm speech Gulliver's comparison of horse-speech to German is a reference to the Emperor Charles V who is supposed to have said that he would 'address his God in Spanish, his mistress in Italian, and his horse in German'

CHAPTER 4 **Gulliver gives an account of his homeland, his arrival, and of the condition of horses in England**

Gulliver's explanation of his arrival makes his master uneasy, because such human activities as doubting, disbelief and lying are unknown to him. At first Gulliver's description of how horses live in England, with Yahoo servants 'to rub their skins smooth, comb their manes, pick their feet' and so on, confirms his belief that 'whatever share of reason the Yahoos pretend to, the Houyhnhnm are your masters'. But Gulliver next explains the use of spurs and the practice of castration. His embarrassment is matched by the 'noble resentment' of his master at this savage treatment. The Houyhnhnm then comments on the disadvantages of Gulliver's physique compared with the local Yahoos, in an argument similar to that of the scholars of Brobdingnag. Beginning to understand what human nature is capable of, the Houyhnhnm asks for an account of Europe and of England.

Much of this chapter explores the nature and use of language, another constant **theme** in the *Travels*. To a rational creature the use of speech is to 'make us understand one another' and to communicate 'facts'. Yet Gulliver, in explaining his own culture, finds himself constantly explaining the meaning of lies and deceit and disputation. What Gulliver tells his master is at first incomprehensible, not least because he requires an enormous vocabulary of vice even to describe his crew, their motivations for travel, and the mutiny. Since this means explaining 'the terrible effects of lust, intemperance, malice and envy', the explanation takes many days.

CHAPTER 5   **Gulliver explains the causes of war, the condition of Europe, and the principles of the English Constitution**

An account of human folly, and especially how wars are fought, leads the Houyhnhnm to his first conclusion about human nature, 'that instead of reason we were only possessed of some quality fitted to increase our natural vices'. Next Gulliver explains the meaning of law, a strange concept to one who believes that 'nature and reason are sufficient guides for a reasonable animal'. Lawyers, Gulliver explains, are trained from youth to prove 'that white is black, and black is white, according as they are paid'. He shows how the law works for nobody's benefit but its own, and explains that as English law is based on precedent, to ensure that whatever has been done once 'may legally be done again', the lawyers 'take special care to record all the decisions formerly made against common justice and the general reason of mankind'.

Gulliver's paragraphs on the causes of war are among the most passionate moments in the *Travels*. As he has done before, he reduces religious controversies (including some Swift took part in) to the point of absurdity, and the motives of princes to utter frivolity. The deadpan style on p. 293 has not been used in quite this way before: now Gulliver divorces words such as 'justifiable', 'lawful' 'honourable' from their general usage, and deduces from the fact that we allow wickedness to be practised the conclusion that we think it good. Is it fair to deduce our values from our conduct? Well, why not? The listing style is used to devastating effect on p. 294, and there is, as usual a special animus in the account of lawyers as not only making a living from systematised falsehood, but as constituting a 'society' to which all others are enslaved.

CHAPTER 6   **The condition of England, continued: exploitation, trade, disease, and quackery. Gulliver's definition of a Minister of State, and of the nobility**

Gulliver turns to an account of the monetary system, by which 'the bulk of our people were forced to live miserably, by labouring every day for small wages to make a few live plentifully'. The cause of this injustice is man's craving for exotic foods and intoxicating liquors and fashionable clothes, which in turn cause 'diseases, folly and vice'. 'Disease' is also a new idea to the Houyhnhnm. An explanation of how men ruin their health leads into a fierce attack on the medical profession which relies partly on the black humour of a list of improbable methods of treating patients, and partly on Gulliver's willingness to slander his own profession. Doctors, he suggests, are quite willing to give a fatal dose, either to please a prince, or simply to make their own gloomy predictions come true. The chapter concludes in **invective** against Ministers of State and the degenerate condition of the nobility.

No summary could convey the force of these passages, which bring together all the fiercest denunciations of human society made throughout the book and intensify them, without a word to suggest that this is any other than the title of the chapter suggests, a plain account of 'the state of England under Queen Anne'.

Gulliver suggests, with deadly **irony**, that all of the social maladies he describes – including venereal disease – constitute a vast *system* contrived and devised by human folly for our own destruction. Human disease, particularly, is the direct consequence of exporting wholesome foods to import noxious substances, eating when we are not hungry and drinking in order to inflame our digestive systems, embracing the sexually polluted, all in order to give business to physicians, whose general remedial system is to proceed in whatever manner is most directly contrary to nature. In the references on pages 300–1 to prostitute female Yahoos and female hypochondria Swift again exposes himself to charges of misogyny.

CHAPTER 7   **Gulliver's Master passes judgement on human nature**

Gulliver excuses his representation of mankind in the previous chapter by saying that his admiration for the virtues of the Houyhnhnms has made him less interested than before in defending the 'honour' of men. Even so, he says, his description was rather biased in favour of his home country. The Houyhnhnm observes that as 'reason alone is sufficient to govern a rational creature' such institutions as government and law are proof that men cannot be rational creatures. They have instead 'a pittance of reason' which they use to increase their corruptions and invent new ones. Gulliver's master makes a lengthy comparison between men and Yahoos, which at first comes as a relief from the **satire** of Chapter 6, but becomes remarkably persuasive.

> You probably found Gulliver's criticisms in Chapters 5 and 6 a little extreme. But can you find any part of the Houyhnhnm's description of the Yahoos, from their fondness for 'shining stones' to their sexual behaviour, which is not a perfectly apt parable of human life? If Gulliver is describing extreme cases, and with great heat, and if the Houyhnhnm's points, made with all courtesy, remind us of normal behaviour, which is the more effective satire? Or is it that the whole point of the crescendo of execration in Chapter 6 was to soften us up for the coup de grace in Chapter 7?

spleen this ailment of the Yahoos, which was common among the fashionable people of Swift's day, is a mixture of low spirits and hypochondria

CHAPTER 8   **Gulliver's observations on the Yahoos, Houyhnhnm Reason, and Houyhnhnm society**

Gulliver sets out to observe the Yahoos, hoping to make more discoveries about human nature. Bathing 'stark naked', he is assaulted by a young female and has to be rescued by his guide. He admits that she was not 'altogether so hideous' as the others, and he appears to take some pride in the fact that she 'stood gazing and howling all the time I was putting on my clothes'. His surprise that she was not a red-head, 'which might have been some excuse' for her lust, is one of many personal attacks Swift made on the red-haired Duchess of Somerset, nicknamed 'Carrots', an old enemy of his at the court of Queen Anne. Returning to his account of the Houyhnhnms, with whom he spent three years in all, he remarks on their 'general disposition to all virtues'. They have no 'opinions', one of the causes of war listed in Chapter 5, and no interest in 'conjectures' because real truths carry 'immediate conviction'. Consequently they have neither disputes nor philosophical arguments. Their qualities of 'friendship and benevolence' are universal, so they have no special family affection. They breed only until each couple has two children, though three are allowed in the servant class to provide domestics for noble families. Marriage is not a matter of passion, but 'one of the necessary actions of a rational being'.

> How attractive is this society? And how possible for humanity? Can you imagine a man of Swift's wit finding residence in a land without opinion or dispute tolerable for one moment? It seems Spartan in its encouragement of physical fitness. Since Houyhnhnm society knows no disputes, Parliament meets for five or six days in every four years to settle unanimously a few items of business such as the fair distribution of oats, cows, Yahoos and children. This last point may strike you as impossibly unfeeling; yet the Houyhnhnm is shocked by the idea that males and females might be educated differently. In this case, 'as he truly observed, one half of our natives were good for nothing but bringing children into the world; and to trust the care of our children to such useless animals, he said, was yet a greater instance of brutality'.

CHAPTER 9   A Houyhnhnm Assembly deliberates on whether to exterminate the Yahoos

The council continues its old debate, 'the only debate which ever happened in that country', as to where the Yahoos came from and whether they should be exterminated. Except for a passage on the

Houyhnhnm attitude to death, which can be read as a comment on Gulliver's experience with the Struldbruggs, the rest of this chapter is made up of brief comments on a number of topics. More space is given to describing their building methods and other examples of their 'dexterity', than to their history, medicine, astronomy and poetry, which are orally transmitted since they have no writing. Gulliver is clearly more interested in their 'not inconvenient' buildings than in their poetry, though in this art, with its just similes and moral sentiments, they 'excel all other mortals'.

Are we meant to observe that the Houyhnhnms are capable of corruption? Gulliver's master, who has learnt a lot from his visitor, suggests gelding the young Yahoos. It is also wise to read this chapter bearing in mind Swift's passion for history, his skill as a writer, his veneration for the 'immortals' of poetry, such as Homer and Shakespeare, and the fact that his own most exuberant poetry, such as 'A Description of a City Shower' is very far from confining itself to just similes and moral sentiments.

CHAPTER 10   **Gulliver's idyllic life with the philosopher horses is terminated by eviction**

A description of Gulliver's life among the Houyhnhnms, a life of simple needs, simply satisfied, sounds all the more attractive in contrast with a list of all the things he was glad to be without – namely people and their follies. His social life consisted of listening humbly to the elevated conversation of his master and his visitors. He comes to loathe even his own reflection and to look on the human race as 'Yahoos in shape and disposition'. A wholehearted convert, Gulliver learns to imitate the Houyhnhnms by trotting like a horse and speaking in their 'voice and manner'. At this point he learns, to his bitter disappointment, that at their last Council the Houyhnhnms had decided that he must leave. His master has reluctantly agreed. So Gulliver sets about building a boat out of wood and Yahoo-skins. He consoles himself for his banishment by planning to persuade mankind to imitate the Houyhnhnms. In an 'extraordinary mark of distinction' his master raises a hoof for Gulliver to kiss.

Gulliver's list of negatives in the long first paragraph is a particularly fine example of what Swift can do with this form: it combines a wonderful list of human follies and vices with an exhilarating sense of rhythm and variety, almost as if Swift's genius is roused to its most brilliant pitch by the denigration of the species. Once again, though, one wonders about the perfection of the horses. How can a Houyhnhnm be reluctant to follow Reason, unless there is, after all, something more to life than Reason? Or is this another suggestion that even Houyhnhnms are corruptible? Unless they are, surely Gulliver is right: it might 'have consisted with Reason to have been less rigorous'.

CHAPTER 11   **Gulliver's expulsion from Houyhnhnmland and his final homecoming**

Hoping to find an uninhabited island where he can spend his days meditating on the Houyhnhnms, Gulliver sets a course toward New Holland. He is attacked by 'savages' at his first landfall and then, against his will, taken on board a Portuguese ship. After a very comical description of Gulliver's stay at the Captain's home in Lisbon he is persuaded to return to England and his family. The sight of them fills him with 'hatred, disgust and contempt' and he swoons when embraced by 'that odious animal' his wife. Five years later he is still unable to touch any of his family: instead he spends four hours a day conversing with his horses, 'who understand me tolerably well'.

In some ways this chapter is remarkably like the last chapter of Part II, in its comic treatment of Gulliver's difficult readjustment, except that on this occasion that difficulty will be permanent: he is permanently irreconcilable to humanity. Don Pedro de Mendez is probably the kindest and most patient person in the book, and everything Gulliver says about him shows us his warm humanity, yet Gulliver condescends only 'to treat him like an animal which had some little portion of reason'.

CHAPTER 12   **Gulliver's farewell to the reader, and discussion of the practicality of colonising the lands he has 'discovered'**

To defend the truth of his record of sixteen years of travelling Gulliver quotes some words of Sinon from Virgil's *Aeneid*, to the effect that 'fortune has made him wretched, but has not made him a liar'. Swift knows, if Gulliver has forgotten, that when Sinon says this he has just told an enormous lie concerning the Trojan horse. But Gulliver's next words are true enough. Who, indeed, can read of the virtuous Houyhnhnms 'without being ashamed of his own vices'? He commends the Brobdingnagians as the least corrupted of Yahoos, and then passes to a discussion of the possibility of colonising any of the countries he has visited.

> Swift's penultimate diatribe, against colonialism, is a powerful instance of his appeal to modern readers: he knew nothing of 'the scramble for Africa', or the East India Company, but it would be hard for a writer with the full history of European imperialism available to compose a fiercer indictment of 'the white man's burden'.

> The final twist needs noticing, too. In the penultimate paragraph, with its attack on human pride, Gulliver and Swift seem unusually at one; but in his closing phrase Gulliver stands alone, the butt of his creator. Throughout Part IV we have the problem of deciding which arguments represent Gulliver's way of thinking, and which Swift's.

> **the Trojan horse** in Book Two of the *Aeneid,* an epic poem by the Roman poet Publius Vergilius Maro (70–19BC), a select band of Greek warriors hid within a gigantic wooden horse, outside the city of Troy which they had besieged. Sinon pretends to be a deserter from the Greek army, and encourages the Trojans to drag the horse into Troy for good luck. At night the Greeks emerge, and take the city

A MODEST PROPOSAL

A MODEST PROPOSAL FOR PREVENTING THE CHILDREN OF
POOR PEOPLE IN IRELAND FROM BEING A BURTHEN TO THEIR
PARENTS OR COUNTRY, AND FOR MAKING THEM BENEFICIAL
TO THE PUBLIC (1729)

SYNOPSIS OF *A MODEST PROPOSAL*

Jonathan Swift's most savage work, *A Modest Proposal*, was inspired by the sufferings of Ireland. In a matter-of-fact style such as any economist might have used, Swift argues that the twin problems of famine and overpopulation could be solved simultaneously by feeding the children of the poor to the households of the rich. The landlords having 'already devoured most of the parents, seem to have the best title to the children'. By 'breeding' especially for the meat market, Ireland could also increase its exports. Swift skilfully turns the screw of horror with each new phase of his argument. In a final hit at English indifference to Irish sufferings he suggests that an added advantage of his proposal is that it runs no danger of 'disobliging England'. Perhaps the most obvious explanation of the cold rage of this short work is that the author of *A Modest Proposal* knew that little more could be expected of a race of Yahoos governed by other Yahoos: one effect of reading *A Modest Proposal* with an eye to its coolly calculated insults to English and Irish alike, is to make one wonder just how much **distance** there was between the author of *Gulliver's Travels* and its misanthropic **narrator**

PAGES 52–3   **Jonathan Swift, in the guise of an economic projector, proposes a simple remedy for Ireland's many problems, including ragged children, impoverished parents, begging, starvation, overpopulation and the excessive number of papists**

Presenting Ireland as a land of poverty, distinguished by a population of begging mothers, each trailed by ragged children, the proposer hints that his scheme will make such children into useful members of the commonwealth. Moreover, it will prevent such abominations as abortion and infanticide, the only remedies currently employed to prevent children growing up into the only profession available to them, that of stealing.

Regretfully, sale of children is no solution, as it would recoup only a quarter of their cost. However, 'a young healthy child well nursed is at a year old a most delicious, nourishing and wholesome food, whether stewed, roasted, baked or boiled'.

Strange jumps in style seem designed to make the reader very unsure of this work's moral bearings. Are the 'strolling' mothers simply walking or street-walking? Is the proposal to 'take in the whole number of infants' ominous or not? How do we negotiate the gap between phrases like 'a child just dropped from its dam', and the idea that infanticide is 'a horrid practice'. Two languages are at work; a moral one, which assumes that the reader can feel pity and shed tears; and an amoral, purely economic one, whose author seems unconscious that to call a child' s mother 'its dam', or classify her as 'a breeder' may give offence. With the moral switch 'on' we are expected to agree that infanticide is deplorable; when it is 'off' we seem to be invited to regard theft as an honourable profession. In between, there is a dead-pan statistical style. The passage computing 120,000 living infants tells us, but without saying so, that only 15 percent of couples in Ireland can support their children, that 85 percent are either beggars or virtually so, and that of these perhaps a third will lose their children through miscarriages or infant mortality. There is more to this writing than a parody of political or bureaucratic language, but that is undoubtedly part of the effect.

the pretender in Spain son of the deposed James II, and 'pretender' to a throne reassigned to William of Orange by the 'Glorious Revolution' of 1688. Swift alludes to a passage in Irish history which still shadows the politics of Northern Ireland

the Barbadoes economic migrants often paid for their passage by becoming bondsmen, or virtual slaves, for lengthy periods

a knowing American the idea that North American Indians practised cannibalism was common in England in the eighteenth-century. Swift may be alluding to early versions of the argument that Ireland, though nominally part of the Kingdom was in reality a colony

PAGES 54–5   A review of the economic benefits of the proposal

The proposer reverts to the language of breeding to consider the marketing of 100,000 twenty-eight pound carcases, each of which will provide four good dishes at a meal with 'particular' friends (particular about their food?) while providing the mother with 8 shillings (40p) net profit, and strengthening the bond between landlord and tenant. Moreover, there will be ancillary benefits; flayed carcases will provide the same gentry with gloves and shoes, and work for butchers, since not all of us will be so particular as to dress the meat 'hot from the knife'. A counter proposal to slaughter twelve year olds, since venison is in short supply, is dismissed as lessening the breeding stock, as well as perhaps bordering upon cruelty. But the proposer admits that 'several plump young girls in this town' would not be missed, if used in this way.

> The rapid passage from the first concrete **image** of a child, 'stewed, roasted, baked or boiled,' to discussion of market economics seems designed as a calculated insult. It is implied that we will not be shocked by the thought of eating, or flaying, or butchering the children of the poor. The moral principle, presumably, is that as we are already guilty of their deaths through disease and starvation, and that doesn't seem to bother us, why should this literal extension from virtual to actual slaughter? But other games are being played. When he hints that the sale of plump, lazy, good-for-nothing, over-dressed, pampered young girls, 'in joints from the gibbet' would not be a bad thing, the animus against these spoilt young parasites may produce a little more assent.

Psalmanazar George Psalmanazar (*c.*1679–1763) was a French impostor who claimed to be a Formosan and described that island's cannibalism

PAGES 56–7   An enumeration of the moral and social benefits of the proposal

Pausing to note that we need not concern ourselves overmuch about the 'aged, diseased, or maimed', since these, along with labourers too weak to labour, dispose of themselves 'as fast as can be reasonably expected', the projector enumerates six advantages: lessening the numbers of papists; helping tenants to pay their rent; adding to gross national domestic product; decreasing the cost of child-rearing; adding to the culinary range of taverns; and proving an inducement to marriage. Having apparently finished his list of advantages, he adds two others. The trade would free up beef and pork for export, and the table arrangements at domestic feasts would be much enhanced by the figure of 'a well-grown, fat, yearling child … roasted whole'.

> This last image is a gratuitous, and surprise, addition. What is the style getting at here? The overall rhetorical arrangement seems to be suggesting that we grow immune to horror so quickly that, if *A Modest Proposal* is to retain any shock value, the projector must give several more turns of the screw. The afterthought that a thousand of us would become constant customers, especially at weddings and christenings, may implicate us in another way: do we deplore the thought more than we relish the joke?

PAGES 57–9   **A comparison of the proposal with other expedients**

The final phase of the *Proposal* assures us that the modest proposal is intended for Ireland alone, and no other kingdom 'that ever was, is, or I think ever can be upon earth'. Swift's projector casually lists some ten 'other expedients' for lessening Ireland's problems; asks what other practical solution there can be to a land where a million 'creatures in human figure' live in beggary, adding to those who are 'beggars by profession' all the farmers, cottagers and labourers who are 'beggars in effect'; and denies that he has any ulterior motive in making his proposal, his wife being past childbearing.

> Perhaps this final passage opens up the real **ambiguity** of *A Modest Proposal*. Despite the gratuitous insult to England, as a land only too willing to devour the whole nation of Ireland, and despite the tragic sense of Irish conditions that comes out sometimes in the style (look at the last sentence of the penultimate paragraph), it can be felt that the real animus in this final passage is against Ireland itself. The 'other expedients' listed here are, in the main, measures Swift had vainly urged on Ireland for years. The whole work portrays Ireland as a land composed of beggars, thieves, layabouts, brutal husbands, indifferent wives, bastard children, cruel landlords,

dishonest shopkeepers, proud, vain, idle women, drunkards and factionalists – in short, as 'creatures in human figure' may imply, as a land of Yahoos. It is a troubling text, not least in the way it expresses the hatred of a patriot for his country.

PART THREE

CRITICAL APPROACHES

Some of the most illuminating comments on *Gulliver's Travels* are those Jonathan Swift made himself, especially in letters to the poet Alexander Pope in September and November 1725 when he was completing the work. In the first letter he said:

> when you think of the world give it one lash the more at my request. I have ever hated all nations, professions and communities, and all my love is towards individuals: for instance I hate the tribe of lawyers, but I love councillor such a one, judge such a one ... but principally I hate and detest that animal called man, although I heartily love John, Peter, Thomas, and so forth.

Referring more specifically to his **theme** he went on:

> I have got materials towards a treatise proving the falsity of that definition *animal rationale* [the definition of man as a rational animal]; and to show it should be only *rationis capax* [capable of reason]. Upon this great foundation of misanthropy ... the whole building of my *Travels* is erected; and I will never have peace of mind till all honest men are of my opinion; by consequence you are to embrace it immediately ...

In November, after another burst of anger – 'Drown the world, I am not content with despising it, but I would anger it if I could with safety' – he added: 'I tell you after all that I do not hate mankind; it is *vous autres* [you others] who hate them, because you would have them reasonable animals, and are angry for being disappointed.' These are fair observations, though Swift did not always spare individuals.

Some later letters are evidence of the high spirits in which Swift published his book. In November 1726, writing to Pope again, he passes on the story that 'A bishop here said that the Part was full of improbable lies, and for his part he hardly believed a word of it'. And in the same month he sent a jesting letter to Henrietta Howard, Countess of Suffolk and his closest friend at court. In this letter he makes several jokes based on his claim that he had never heard of *Gulliver's Travels* and could not understand her allusions to it until he received a copy. Then he rejects her offer to pay for some materials she has asked for:

> the weaver ... has no conception of what you mean by returning money, for he is become a proselyte of the Houyhnhnms, whose great principle (if I rightly remember) is benevolence. And as to myself, I am rightly affronted with such a base proposal that I am determined to complain of you to Her Royal Highness, that you are a mercenary Yahoo fond of shining pebbles. ... I am not such a prostitute flatterer as Gulliver; whose chief study is to extenuate the vices and magnify the virtues of mankind, and perpetually dins our ears with praises of his country in the midst of corruptions, and for that reason alone hath found so many readers; and probably will have a pension, which I suppose was his chief design in writing. As for his compliments to the ladies, I can easily forgive him as a natural effect of that devotion which our sex always ought to pay to yours.

Apart from showing that at least one of the Maids of Honour could enjoy court **satires**, Swift's references in this letter to Gulliver's 'flattery' is a very helpful comment on his relation to Gulliver. Clearly, Swift did set out to vex the 'world', by which he probably meant the world of politicians in particular, and of leaders of social and intellectual fashion. Equally clearly, however, he knew that his own exuberant sense of humour was shared by those for whose good opinion he really cared.

THE QUESTION OF GENRE

GULLIVER'S TRAVELS AS A NOVEL

In some ways *Gulliver's Travels* is a unique work: there is nothing *quite* like it in world literature. But it shares certain features with many famous works, including religious and philosophical allegories, **Utopias**, travel books, romances, adventure novels and comic fiction. Have pity on the librarian deciding how to classify it: generally, you will find it under fiction, but quite often under miscellaneous prose. At times, especially in the opening sections of each of the *Travels*, it reminds one of the straightforward narrative of Defoe's *Robinson Crusoe* (1719). Some later eighteenth-century classics such as Dr Johnson's *Rasselas* (1759), Fielding's *Tom Jones* (1749), and Smollett's *Roderick Random* (1748) all share features of Swift's style. Clearly Swift's Part is in the tradition of masterly storytelling. But is it a novel, like these works of Defoe, Fielding and Smollett, with a plot and a hero?

Some critics find that there is a developing story in *Gulliver's Travels,* and not merely a record of four voyages. It is the story of a man who undergoes a series of experiences in a significant order, which in a novel would result either in the education of that man, or in his downfall. His four journeys are subtly different, especially in the way they begin and end. His shipwreck in Lilliput is a mere accident, and he returns home in good company and comfort. In Brobdingnag his shipmates desert him, and the whole experience of his stay in that land affects his behaviour for months. Pirates and a malicious Dutchman abandon him to his fate near Laputa, and when his disturbing experiences there are over he sails home in a Dutch ship in continual fear for his life. The mutiny which opens Part IV is clearly the last straw and so we are psychologically prepared for his rejection of mankind at the end.

So much for his experiences. What of the man who experiences them? We are sure enough at the start about our trustworthy **narrator**. His qualities of resourcefulness and truthfulness, his general decency and his sense of honour as a gentleman are in no doubt. But as the work progresses we may note some less desirable features: his pride, his anxiety to please, his moral callousness, his patronising attitudes to real superiority. We know from Chapter 2 (Part I) that he suffers from weak eyes, but it is his moral vision that fails him most often. The closer you look, the more inconsistent he becomes. As the book progresses he seems less and less able to distinguish right from wrong. In Laputa he effectively disappears, in that he has no reliable core of personality left. (In the chapter summaries in Part 2 you will find many illustrations of all these points, and you should look for your own examples).

In the end these characteristics may make us doubt his existence as a real character. Although the book looks like a novel its real purpose is satire, and Gulliver is not only *not the author* of his book, he is *not even a character* in it, though he sometimes resembles one. Gulliver must be whatever Swift needs him to be at each turn in the satire. Occasionally he must be real enough for us to trust him, but only so that he may mislead us into one of Swift's satirical traps. In one thing, however, he is consistent. Unlike Swift he lacks the slightest sense of humour, despite attempting a foolish pun on one or two occasions. He lacks any consciousness of **irony**, as he must if the reader is to do the work of interpretation. A plain blunt fellow at the start, he ends up with very little self-understanding. Of all possible readers Gulliver would be the least able to appreciate the ironic art of 'saying the thing that is not'.

GULLIVER'S TRAVELS AND OTHER GENRES

Swift's friend Dr Arbuthnot made an interesting comparison in welcoming the appearance of *Gulliver's Travels*. 'I will make over all my profits to you for the property of *Gulliver's Travels*, which I believe, will have as great a run as John Bunyan.' John Bunyan (1628–88) was the author of *The Pilgrim's Progress* (1678), which puts the values of English Protestantism into the form of a vivid story. While it would be hard to read *Gulliver's Travels* as religious **allegory** in the same sense as Bunyan's work – it hardly sets out to convey a sense of the Christian life – one can see it is an allegorical attack on the eighteenth-century belief that man, as a rational being, could get on very well without God. Another **genre** with which *Gulliver's Travels* shares a great deal (and superficially even more) is the travel book, whether fictional or factual. Imaginative literature often takes this form. Lucian's *True History*, in the second century AD, was probably the first parody of the traveller's tale as such. Classical epic, such as Homer's *Odyssey*, and eighteenth-century picaresque fiction, such as Fielding's *Tom Jones* (1749) and Smollett's *Roderick Random* (1748), tend to be constructed as a series of instructive adventures.

The hero of *Robinson Crusoe*, which is an attempt at realist fiction on this theme, shares many of Gulliver's characteristics. Daniel Defoe (1661–1731) based his hero on Alexander Selkirk who had actually been rescued from the island of Juan Fernandez in 1711 by the explorer William Dampier. Swift is engaged in deliberate parody both of Defoe's fiction and of Dampier's accounts of genuine travels. He not only parodies the style of Dampier's records, *A New Voyage round the World* (1697) and *A Voyage to New Holland* (1703–9), but arranges the dates of Gulliver's 'discoveries' of Lilliput, Brobdingnag, Laputa and Houyhnhnmland to coincide with Dampier's presence in the appropriate latitudes. The painstaking way in which Swift mimics the style of such writers in the narrative parts of the *Travels* is illustrated by the storm scene at the start of Part II, (which Swift took word for word from a sailor's publication in 1679). Except that it seems funnier, because it is more densely packed with nautical jargon, one would scarcely detect any difference from Gulliver's usual manner of narration.

Accounts of travels are also associated with the **Utopian** genre. The opening of Sir Thomas More's *Utopia* (1516), and that of Cyrano de Bergerac's *Histoire Comique contenant les états et empires de la Lune* (1657), are parodies of a similar kind. But *Gulliver's Travels* is both a thorough parody of the travel tale and a book made up of several competing Utopias. The search for the perfect society is a perpetual theme of literature, and Plato's *Republic,* More's *Utopia,* Butler's *Erewhon* (1871), Huxley's *Brave New World* (1932) and Orwell's *1984* (1949) are only the most famous examples of the genre, depicting visions or nightmares of what the world might be. Swift's Part gives us four or five to choose from, with the added spice that because of his **ironic** technique we can never be sure whether we are in a 'Utopia' or not. Finally, what we have in *Gulliver's Travels* is an extended analysis of the political and intellectual world of man, an **'anatomy'** of society by means of allegory, and an investigation of moral issues by means of many short parables embedded in the work. All the works you will find listed under 'Allegory' or 'Parable' in a dictionary of literary terms have some bearing on this work.

Of all these genres, the most pertinent, perhaps, is the Utopia. Every so often in *Gulliver's Travels,* amid chapters of innocent narrative, flights of invention, and satirical attacks, we catch a glimpse of something that reminds us of man's perpetual quest for Utopia. Part of the challenge of reading the book is trying to detect which of several Utopias is the real one. The more ambitious examples of the ideal social structure often turn out to be a satire on mankind's grandiose dreams: a perfect world is not a possibility for man, and Swift knows it. In the *Travels* it is usually the more moderate proposals that carry most conviction, the appeals to common decency and common sense. The opening paragraph of Part III, Chapter 6, describing, ironically, some the 'impossible' ideas of the school of political projectors, or the passages in Part II, describing the modest achievements of the Brobdingnagian state, seem to illustrate a practical ideal for man to aim at.

POLITICAL ALLEGORY

Behind the charming story of Gulliver's adventures in Lilliput lies a systematic allegory of political events, though this has been differently interpreted. One theory is that of Sir Charles Firth who argued that Lilliput was first written as a Utopia, with Gulliver getting into a few scrapes which should be interpreted autobiographically, and was later revised into an allegory of Whig/Tory politics, at which point Gulliver represents the Earl of Oxford and Viscount Bolingbroke. So the story of the palace fire which Gulliver extinguishes so improperly is assumed to refer to the Queen's prejudice against Swift himself. Her enmity was encouraged by the Earl of Nottingham, among others, who appears in this Part as Bolgolam, Admiral of the Realm, and a man of 'morose and sour complexion'. Nottingham did in fact have a remote connection with naval affairs, and Swift's name for the morose earl, in two earlier ballads, was 'Dismal'. Reldresal, in this autobiographical interpretation, is Lord Carteret, Principal Secretary of State in 1721–4, and a friend of Swift. In 1724 Carteret was made Lord Lieutenant of Ireland and had the unpleasant task of offering a reward for information as to the identity of the author of the *Drapier's Letters*. In Lilliput, Reldresal has to suggest a punishment for Gulliver.

    A. E. Case sees the whole of Part I as a consistent allegory of the persecution of Oxford and Bolingbroke by the new Whig ministry after the death of Queen Anne. So the fire represents the War of the Spanish succession, settled by the Tories in illegal negotiations with France. Bolgolam is certainly Nottingham, but identifiable as such by Nottingham's known hostility to Oxford. Reldresal is Viscount Townshend, a Whig who pretended to befriend Bolingbroke and Oxford. Gulliver's flight to Blefuscu is Bolingbroke's flight to France, and so on. Case identifies a whole series of minor characters and asserts the total consistency of the allegory given that the reigns of Anne and George are combined in Gulliver's tale by making them Emperor and Empress. All commentators agree, incidentally, that Flimnap is Walpole, who by 1726 was effectively Britain's first Prime Minister, but who had been a leading enemy of the Tories as early as 1715, and became head of government in 1720. Chapter 3 of Part I can be read as a portrait of George's court under Walpole's ministry, Chapter 4 as a general account of England and a history of its factions, Chapter 5 as an allegory of the War of the Spanish Succession, Chapter 7 as referring to the impeachment of the Tory leaders, and Chapter 8 as beginning with Bolingbroke's escape to France.

Politically, the method of Part II is quite different. The events of Lilliput, that is, the whole history of **Augustan** England, are compressed into a paragraph or so of Gulliver's first audience with the king, who 'after a hearty fit of laughing, asked me whether I were a Whig or a Tory'. The wisdom of this king marks him as one of Swift's portraits of the ideal monarch. Indeed Chapter 7 as a whole is one of Swift's clearest statements of a positive political ideal. The hint at the end of this chapter that Brobdingnag has known its own political disorder makes it all the clearer that the stability and simplicity of the Brobdingnagian state is meant as a model for England to imitate.

In Part III, Swift returns to a detailed political allegory. But where Lilliput tells the story of how Oxford and Bolingbroke fell from power, in Laputa the satire is directed against the state of affairs in the 1720s. The target now is the Whig-dominated court of George I. The decay and disintegration of Balnibarbi, the British Isles, under the rule of a remote court and newfangled Whig policies (as opposed to traditional conservative prudence), is blended with a detailed allegory of Irish resistance to Walpole's policies. The court of the flying island is easy to identify as that of George I, for King George was a connoisseur of music and his reign was one in which a variety of sciences, notably astronomy, were encouraged. The Prince of Wales also reappears. In Lilliput he had one heel higher than the other because he was inclined to the Tories. In Laputa he is the 'great lord at court, closely related to the King' who befriends Gulliver, and who is sympathetically presented as interested in practical affairs, able to do without a 'flapper', and well-disposed towards Lord Munodi. Munodi, the former Governor of Lagado, is now in disgrace and lives a quiet life on his country estate, the only part of the realm which is properly run. Of course Munodi is a portrait of Swift's friend Oxford, who had retired after surviving the Whigs' attempt to impeach him. Perhaps Swift hoped that in the next reign Oxford would be restored to office. Certainly the allegory can be read this way. Even Bolingbroke reappears briefly, in Chapter 6, in the passage where 'our brother Tom has just got the piles' is treated as an **anagram** for 'Resist; a plot is brought home; The tour'. Swift is making a general reference to the belief that Jacobite conspirators corresponded in anagrams, and a specific reference to Bolingbroke who was known in France as Monsieur La Tour.

That Swift's contemporaries could recognise a very precise and ingenious allegory of recent events, in Part I and in Part III, is true. But Swift's approach means that what was vivid and meaningful in 1726 will remain so in 2026. The story is quite unblemished by baffling **allusions**. It is a perfect cover story for Swift's hidden meanings, enjoyable in itself, and capable of illuminating our own time as mercilessly as it did his. It is arguable that by concentrating on specific historical references we miss the real power of the *Travels* as a satire on man in all ages. In any case, the work is so written that each Part can be enjoyed simultaneously as a story, as moral satire, and as political satire.

Oddly, it is a political satire that can be enjoyed by people of quite different persuasions. Despite his own fiercely partisan activities, Swift believed that he was lending his support to those who stood for common sense and common interests, against Tory Jacobites at one stage of his career, and against the power of Whig financial interests later on. His satire on political corruption is not based on a particular ideology, but on a hatred of absolute power. His treatment of war and of standing armies is similarly based. For armies can be made the instruments either of internal tyranny or of imperial conquests, and both tyranny and empire are powerfully criticised in this work. Conservative though he was, there are several issues of this kind where Swift seems to stand in the vanguard of progressive opinion. His views on the education of women, and his attack on the exploitation of the many to enrich the few (Part IV, Chapters 8 and 6) mark him as a radical spirit, ahead of his time. Yet twice in the book he displays a fierce intolerance towards religious dissenters, and his Commonwealth of horses (as Orwell complained) has as rigid a class structure, and as little tolerance of diversity of thought, as the most reactionary of regimes.

Here is a quotation from Swift's autobiographical 'Verses on the Death of Dr Swift':

> *Perhaps I may allow the Dean,*
> *Had too much satire in his vein;*
> *And seemed determined not to starve it,*
> *Because no age could more deserve it.*
> *Yet malice never was his aim;*
> *He lashed the vice but spared the name;*
> *No individual could resent,*
> *Where thousands equally were meant;*
> *His satire points at no defect,*
> *But what all mortals may correct; ...*

Does Swift satirise only 'what all mortals may correct? Many readers, in the nineteenth century and in the twentieth, have doubted this. When we have analysed the objects of his satire there is always the uncomfortable feeling that much of his energy, and much of what makes his work genuinely disturbing, arose from his willingness to satirise not only human follies, but 'the human condition'. *Gulliver's Travels* does appear to criticise man for having natural functions, appetites and anxieties. The satire in some places may strike you as excessively fierce. And you should consider Aldous Huxley's opinion that Swift 'could never forgive man for being a vertebrate mammal as well as an immortal soul'.

SATIRE AS MIRROR

As Swift said in his preface to *The Battle of the Books*: 'Satire is a sort of glass wherein beholders do generally discover everybody's face but their own; which is the chief reason ... that so very few are offended with it'. *Gulliver's Travels* comes as close as any work in English literature to disproving Swift's **ironic** comments on the limits of his art. Reading it is like participating in a game in which the satirist is manipulating the mirror and the reader is constantly trying to avoid seeing his own reflection. The moments in which we are 'diverted' by seeing in that mirror comic or libellous distortions of everyone about us will always outnumber the fleeting moments of vexation when we catch sight of ourselves. But Swift is not easy to elude. He is as agile a player of the satire game as anyone, and this section can only outline some of the tricks of which he is capable.

We all know that irony means 'saying one thing while meaning another'. But of course the irony is wasted unless the reader in fact grasps what is meant as well as what is said. Irony is one of the ways we communicate with each other, either for mutual entertainment, or in jokes at the expense of a third party, or sometimes with genuine hostility. Dramatists use a version of irony in which author and audience are in possession of knowledge which at least one of the characters on stage does not have. When we get the sense that Swift is cordially inviting us to share a joke at Gulliver's expense, something similar comes into play. In a work of satire written in fictional form, that is, with a plot and a hero, we can expect to find many refinements of both verbal and situational (or dramatic) irony. In *Gulliver's Travels,* where **allegory** and parable are also employed, the range of possible ironic effects is almost infinite.

GULLIVER AS AN IRONIC DEVICE

Gulliver himself is Swift's most versatile device. His narration is so apparently innocent of malice that our guard is weakened from the outset. His polite and agreeable manner insures us against betrayal, yet he is the cause of most of our confusion. His shortcomings are always involving us in absurdities. The innocent pleasure with which he records that his 'clemency' to the Lilliputians in Chapter 2 was 'represented very much to my advantage at court' (p. 66) identifies us with his ludicrous anxiety to be well thought of in that quarter, just as his surprise at the King of Brobdingnag's 'unnecessary scruple' about gunpowder shows how Swift takes for granted our indifference to human life. Sometimes Swift betrays Gulliver alone for comic effect, sometimes he betrays us through Gulliver. His tendency to make Gulliver give us a superficial view of things, as he does of the political games in the Lilliputian court, exploits the time-lag, perhaps only a split second, between reading Gulliver's words and detecting Swift's meaning. At other times Gulliver is liable to defend us so ineptly against some monstrous criticism that his defence only underlines the criticism, for instance when he says in Part IV that he was unable to prove that human beings are relatively clean since there were no pigs in that country to compare us with.

LOCATING THE AUTHOR

The shifting relation between Swift and Gulliver is never quite predictable. In Chapter 3 of Part II the king clearly speaks for Swift as he contemplates Gulliver: 'and yet, said he, I dare engage, these creatures have their titles and distinctions of honour, they contrive little nests and burrows ... they love, they fight, they cheat, they betray' (p. 146). We may share Gulliver's blushes at this point. We may resent such contempt, perhaps more deeply than we regret the vices named by the king. Sometimes Swift exploits his **mask** in a joke about himself, as he does near the end of the work when Gulliver claims that 'I meddle not the least with any *party*, but write without passion prejudice or ill-will against any man or number of men whatsoever' (p. 342). More often Gulliver is made to reverse his moral stance too quickly for us to evade the trap, as in the transition from Chapter 5 to Chapter 6 of Part III. If you look carefully at this passage you will see that there is in fact a *double* trap. It takes a moment to realise that in the first paragraph of Chapter 6 Gulliver has involved us in a contemptuous rejection of what is most desirable. And it takes a further moment to realise that when these excellent projects are dismissed as 'wild impossible chimeras that never entered before into the heart of man' (p. 232) Swift may well be suggesting that man really *is* so incorrigible that such sensible proposals really *are* too wild to engage our hearts.

VERBAL IRONY

In most of these instances we see Swift exploiting the variable status of his fictional 'author'. But his own favourite verbal ironies are equally various. The use of **hyperbole**, praise so inflated that we know it to be ironically deflating, is a frequent device in Part I. It is used, for instance, in the opening description of the Emperor, which is composed of every grace and feature that George I certainly did not possess, and later in the splendid invocation to that same six-inch Emperor as 'Delight and terror of the universe ... monarch of all Monarchs' (p. 79). A similar use of this technique of reversal is used more seriously in Gulliver's own praise of the virtues of his country throughout Part II.

More subtle is Swift's habit of leaving something unsaid. What is left out is usually the most important dimension, the moral issue. This can take the form of a report on the Lilliputian debate about how to dispose of Gulliver. Or it can appear in passages like the discussion in Part IV of the causes of war, for instance 'whether the juice of a certain *berry* be *blood* or *wine*' (p. 292). This way of seeing religious wars is reductive: the issues are misrepresented by taking the symbols of the Christian sacrament at their face value. But the paragraph that follows lists more examples of the causes of wars. These sound equally ridiculous and contemptible, and they *are* contemptible. The technique remains the same, but we have to read the two paragraphs rather differently, and the second makes us reconsider the first. Such calls on our discrimination are frequently made in another of Swift's favourite games, the catalogue. The list of ways in which men make a living – 'begging, robbing, stealing, ... voting, scribbling, stargazing, poisoning, whoring, canting, libelling, freethinking and the like occupations' (p. 299) – leaves us to decide whether to discriminate between prostitution, journalism, astronomy, politics, or theft as occupations befitting a rational and virtuous being. One consequence of such varied rhetorical techniques is that when, at the end of Part II, Chapter 6, the King of Brobdingnag makes his judgement on the human race, we are so grateful for a plain, direct, way of putting things that we are the more disposed to accept what he says as the plain unvarnished truth.

SITUATIONAL SATIRE

Swift's irony is not only a matter of words. The whole conception of the story serves an **ironic** purpose. How long is it, in Part I, before we realise that Gulliver is not (or not always) an Englishman in a strange land of mannikins but that the mannikins are ourselves and Gulliver the outsider? He is, luckily, a rather naive outsider or his critique would be more bitter than it is. In Brobdingnag, however, Gulliver remains embarrassingly human. He puts the case for man with all the eloquence at his command, but in a series of innocent rhetorical questions his virtuous host exposes the thorough corruption of our world. That effect is all the more terrifying in the final Part, of course, where Gulliver's attempt to explain man to a creature entirely innocent of what may be meant by opinion, doubt or sickness, let alone wealth, fraud or deceit, puts us all on the rack of situational satire.

EMOTIONAL SHOCK

At times Swift finds other ways to embarrass us. Notice how the sexual fantasy of Chapter 5 in Part II, which plays upon the reader's fascination with the body in close-up, is followed directly by another close-up, of the decapitation of a murderer. Transitions of this kind play cruelly on the reader's weaknesses. The appeal to our longing for immortality is a similar bait in the Struldbrugg parable. We are sometimes in a trap that is not merely an ironic game but on the verge of surrealist nightmare, a nightmare that reaches peaks of grotesque imagination in Part III. Our guide may still be an eighteenth-century gentleman, but so was the 'author' of Swift's A *Tale of a Tub* who made that famous aside, 'Last week I saw a woman flayed, and you will hardly believe how much it altered her person for the worse'. There are few shocks in the cinema of violence or theatre of cruelty that Swift did not anticipate.

INVECTIVE

It is a relief, in a way, to have to deal with one of Swift's/Gulliver's straightforward flights of **invective**. These range from the description in Part III of England as a land of informers, to the furious onslaught on the entire legal profession in Part IV. We know, or hope, that not all lawyers are as Gulliver describes them, but we may also feel that such savage indignation is fully justified. Swift is protesting, on behalf of humanity, against ills we need not suffer from but for the greed, malice, or indifference, of those who really scorn their fellow men.

RELATIVITY

Unfortunately Swift does not leave us with this rather comfortable enjoyment of seeing our common enemies given a thorough verbal thrashing. There are effects of *Gulliver's Travels* that strike at us all. Consider the structure once again. If the 'nobility' of Lilliputians is contemptible because of their size, or the beauty of a young woman becomes repulsive when magnified to Brobdingnagian proportions, do not these effects leave us with a sense that perhaps all beauty, or value, or dignity, is relative? Is everything we value so meaningless? Is any ground left for our self-esteem? These effects are not wholly negative, though some readers have found them so. Decency remains decency on whatever scale. The problem is to find the few qualities that are not shown to be relative. When we have found those we have found Swift's positives, the firm base from which he launches his ironic missiles.

MAJOR STRUCTURAL IRONIES

Reading Parts I to III successfully still leaves us with problems in Part IV. Here all Swift's arts are employed to their best effect. The narrative is brilliantly devised. Gulliver's recognition of himself as Yahoo is so thoroughly convincing that we have to share his despairing admiration of the Houyhnhnms and desire to emulate them. We may feel at the end that we cannot be Houyhnhnms, and that Gulliver is the victim of a delusion rather than a revelation. But we cannot avoid feeling that our kinship with the Yahoos is inescapable. Man is not, as we would like to believe, the perfection of nature, but an animal with some tincture of reason. For Swift's contemporaries that was an instructive joke. For the nineteenth century it was an obscene libel. But all readers must feel something of Gulliver's identification.

How is this done? It is achieved by the most sustained piece of rhetoric in Part IV. Chapters 4, 5 and 6 are perhaps the most savage indictment of humanity ever written. It is surely the effect of reading some twenty pages of unrestrained libel on the species that makes us fall so eagerly into the trap Swift has set for us. Chapter 7 is a deceptively calm interlude. Gulliver's master reflects a little on what he has heard, and begins to make a few interesting observations on the Yahoos. There is no malice in this anthropological account of our species, but the effect is profound. Few of us will have taken Gulliver's ferocious account of certain classes of men as a fair account of ourselves: for one thing, we are not, most of us, ministers, nobles or lawyers. But if Swift allows us to dissent from this savage picture he does so in order that we shall willingly recognise ourselves in what follows. The Houyhnhnm's calm account of

SWIFT'S IRONY continued

the Yahoos is a description, through parables, of the ordinary moral qualities of ordinary men, and we believe every word of it.

STYLE & LANGUAGE

The first four paragraphs of Part I are a model of economy. For the child reader what matters is that after four paragraphs Gulliver has set sail, and after another three sentences has been shipwrecked. But the adult reader has noticed that the hero is an educated man, a graduate of Cambridge and Leiden, skilled in medicine, mathematics and languages, that he is much travelled. We also notice that he married the second daughter of 'Mr Edmond Burton, hosier in Newgate Street, with whom I received four hundred pounds'. How remarkably open and frank our **narrator** is, and how carefully he names three employers and gives four addresses. If he were not so brief he would be a thoroughly tedious pedant. It takes some skill to suggest a dull and cautious man in so few words.

By the end of the fifth paragraph we are in a different world and Gulliver is the prisoner of the Lilliputians. Read that paragraph very closely and you will learn a lot about Gulliver as a man and Swift as a writer. In twenty lines Gulliver reaches Van Diemen's Land, his ship is wrecked and he loses his companions. We know the latitude, the state of the weather, the date, the condition of the crew and we might be reading a ship's log. As Gulliver tells us of his experience he omits no detail, for instance, how much he drank before leaving the ship, a necessary preparation for his first spectacular urination. He takes scrupulous care to assert nothing that he does not know to be the exact truth: 'We rowed by my computation about three leagues'. He 'conjectured' it was eight in the evening. There were no houses or at least he was too weak to 'observe them'. Gulliver is not the man to say 'I slept better than I ever did in my life', rather he must write 'sounder than ever I remember to have done'. Read the paragraph down to 'I perceived it to be a human creature not six inches high' (p. 56) and observe just how many touches of that kind have convinced us that Gulliver is the soul of honour, incapable of a word of exaggeration or a voluntary departure from the truth in every particular.

The most rapid strokes of narrative, the descriptions of places and persons, the reported conversations, are all in the same medium: clear, terse, 'masculine', free of elaborate constructions, down-to-earth. It is the style of a man of plain words and common sense. Yet this style is made the vehicle of complex effects of irony, and it has to serve two 'authors', Gulliver with his vision of things as they seem, and Swift with his determination to show us things as they are. As the **satirical** purpose builds, however, language is used rather differently. The contests for coloured 'ribbons' reduce to absurdity the noble orders of the Garter, the Thistle and the Bath. Flimnap, a fine leaper and creeper, is mentioned in this connection for a specific reason. For the order of the Bath (the red ribbon) was created by Walpole as a consolation prize for those who had failed to win the Garter. Here the ridiculous and the actual (ribbons, garters) or the literal and **metaphorical** (leaping and creeping) sit side by side. Such blending of effects is characteristic. The language of the first paragraph of Lilliput's Imperial proclamation (p. 79) is a noteworthy blend of comedy and sublimity. 'Mully Ullu Gue' is hard to pronounce without a chuckle, and 'Five thousand blustrugs (about twelve miles)' compresses two ways of indicating bluster. Yet the poetic prose and biblical cadences of 'Monarch of all Monarchs ... dreadful as winter' is genuinely sublime. Compare this with the Articles of Impeachment, pp. 104–5, where the combination of plain truth and political varnish effects a deadly parody of legal and constitutional language and morality.

Swift sometimes combines his delight in the possibilities of metaphor, and the absurd fallacies that can arise from reasoning by **analogy**, with an equal delight in juxtaposing high topics, such as statesmanship, with distinctly base ones, such as excrement. In Part III Chapter 6, he plays several games based on the analogy between the physical body and the body politic. One such game is a fine instance of his listing style. Senatorial occupational hazards include such ailments as 'spleen, flatus, vertigos and deliriums; with scrofulous tumours full of fetid purulent matter; with sour frothy ructations, with canine appetites and crudeness of digestion' (p. 233) for which combination of probable and improbable disorders the treatment (at the close of each day's debate) should include: 'lenitives, aperitives, abstersives, corrosives, restringents, palliatives, laxatives, cephalalgics, icterics, apophlegmatics, acoustics, as their several cases required' (p. 233). Here Swift combines actual medical terms with comical inventions and **malapropisms**, running them together so as to make the real and the imaginary, the scientific and the bogus, seem inseparable. The teasing concoction charges the whole profession with quackery.

Since politicians are easy game in almost any time and culture, one remedy for political inertia is described with particular gusto. As a corrective to short and weak memories, the doctors propose 'that whoever attended a first minister, after having told his business with the utmost brevity, and in the plainest words, should at his departure give the said minister a tweak by the nose, or a kick in the belly, or tread on his corns, or lug him thrice by both ears, or run a pin into his breech, or pinch his arm black and blue, to prevent forgetfulness: and at every levee day repeat the same operation, till the business were done or absolutely refused' (p. 233–4). Again, there is broad humour in the conjunction of vigorous and offensive language with dignified persons, but Swift's slapstick is offering the reader, vicariously, the satisfactions of gross physical aggression. The language seems designed to involve us in the bawdy and bring out, perhaps, our own Yahoo dispositions. Perhaps the surcharge of aggression is there to diagnose, while it appeals to, our ultimate distrust of reason and of rulers, our distaste for order, and our capacity for violence.

STRUCTURE & THEME

Swift **satirises** throughout this work what he sees as the dangerous illusion of man's perfectibility, or the idea that man is a rational animal. He treats with a surprising even-handedness a variety of political ideas, and factions. He is objective enough to make fun of religious intolerance, even of kinds that he shared. He is one of the great anti-war writers, and his treatment of human ambition and expansionism extends to passages that seem fiercely critical of colonialism and imperialism. He treats man's fear of death, and desire for immortality. His scepticism about progress includes even scientific progress: much of the work suggests that post-renaissance science is more prone to error than that of the ancients, and Laputa, especially, appears to inaugurate the modern theme of science employed to maim and enslave rather than to aid human development. He treats with unparalleled scorn the hereditary nobility. He supports the education of women. The structure of *Gulliver's Travels* suggests, however, that certain key themes are primary: human reason and human pride.

BIG MEN AND LITTLE MEN

What satirical use does Swift make of the relatively simple idea, as Dr Johnson said 'of big men and little men'? At first, Swift seems deliberately to leave us in doubt about the effect of the reverse of scale when we pass from Part I to Part II. We may share Gulliver's anxiety when he sees his first Brobdingnagian, even if we remember the groundlessness of the Lilliputians' similar fear in Part I: 'for, as human creatures are observed to be more savage and cruel in proportion to their bulk, what could I expect but to be a morsel in the mouth of the first of these enormous barbarians' (p. 125). Indeed Gulliver does encounter great dangers and suffers at the hands of jealous dwarfs and greedy peasant-farmers.

The change of scale also introduces a note of disgust which did not appear in Part I. The Brobdingnagians are frequently repulsive, whether Gulliver is describing the nurse in Chapter 1 suckling a baby, or the beggars in Chapter 4. Swift's attack on human vanity is impressive, and because it is increasingly personal it is disturbing. It is the *behaviour* of Lilliputians that makes them, in the end, contemptible. It is the *size* of the nurse's nipple that makes her repulsive. We have to deal with these two **images**, the nurse and the beggars, very differently. Since we are not in Gulliver's position we would be morally deformed if we saw each other as he sees the nurse. But in the case of the beggars is it not the point that we are morally deformed if we do *not* see them as he does? In the first case Dr Swift has diagnosed a case of vanity: he shows us ourselves in grotesque close-up. In the second, he diagnoses a case of moral myopia and he describes the state of the beggars by magnifying their lice and their cancers until our disgust matches his own. Swift was affected by sights of this kind. Most of us have a convenient faculty of not seeing what might disturb us. In *A Tale of a Tub* Swift called it the faculty 'of being well deceived, the serene peaceful state of being a fool among knaves'.

Some of the effects of the change of scale are predictable. The humour of Gulliver's feats in Lilliput is matched by the humour of his calamities in Brobdingnag, where the defiler of a Lilliputian palace ends up wading through cow-dung, and the captor of a Blefuscudian fleet is given a boat which can be hung on a nail to dry. Less obvious is the relation between the modes of satire. Where in Lilliput George I is mocked by a flattering description, in Brobdingnag the Maids of Honour, 'excellent ladies for whom I have all manner of respect', are attacked in an account of their morals which relies on polite understatement and assumed innocence to suggest that immorality is only natural in ladies of the court.

The scale of the Lilliputians is an optical trick, and it calls attention to what we see. It is clear that while matters like the attractiveness of the Lilliputians, and the absurdities of their attempts at dignified behaviour, are noticed by us all as readers, Gulliver as **narrator** only sees the first. He is unable to see how ludicrous his own humility looks in this context, or how comic is the pride he takes in his title of 'Nardac'. But if we agree that Gulliver's humility is comic, haven't we fallen into a moral trap? Parts I and II seem designed to make it as hard as possible to remember all the time that morality and decent behaviour are in no way connected with size. Of course we all know that, and we all recognise that when in Part II Gulliver assumes that the Brobdingnagians must be barbarians because they are enormous, he is comically wrong. Yet we must all share the feeling, throughout Part I, that (a) these people are comic because they are tiny, (b) they ought to be good because they are so tiny, and (c) their wickedness is especially shocking because they are so tiny. We, of course, being bigger, may be forgiven somewhat bigger sins. At least, that is what Swift may expect us to feel.

So this simple idea of little men and big men is really very ingenious, and the invention may have a deeper purpose in terms of the *Travels* as a whole. It may make us realise in the end that while we think we are rational and moral beings we can be thrown into moral confusion by a simple change of scale. A further effect is to show us how easily we become prejudiced, how rapidly we make a moral judgement about a person or a nation and then expect everything we learn about them subsequently to conform to our own preconceptions or first impressions. Read any two or three consecutive pages from Chapter 6 of Part I (or Chapter 3 of Part II, or Chapter 8 of Part IV) and see how many times your opinion of the 'host' people has to change. So Swift uses scale as one of his techniques of disorientation or betrayal, to show us two things. First, how erratic and variable our moral judgements are. And second, how easily our notions become fixed and prejudiced. Would you agree that both these statements are true, and that they appear to be contradictory?

LAPUTA, GLUBBDUBDRIB AND LUGGNAGG: THE THEME OF IMPROVEMENT

People have always argued about the success of Part III. Made up of several short episodes it lacks the unity of the other voyages. And considered simply as a story there is one important factor missing. Gulliver is not involved, as hero, in events of compelling narrative interest. Children usually like this Part the least and most critics agree with them. Yet Swift felt that the third voyage was needed to make a transition between the two **Utopian** Parts, Brobdingnag and the Houyhnhnms, and as he wrote it last, and for this purpose, Part III is in fact carefully linked both to Lilliput and to Brobdingnag in theme, and to Houyhnhnmland through the character of Gulliver. It is linked to Lilliput by the return to detailed political **allegory**. It is linked to Brobdingnag by an intellectual theme, and by playing the game of reversal in an intellectual rather than a physical dimension. We may remember, as we read of the Laputan astronomers and the projectors of Lagado, one of the most quoted remarks of the King of Brobdingnag, who says in Chapter 7 that 'whoever could make two ears of corn ... grow on a spot of ground where only one grew before, would deserve better, of mankind, and do more essential service to his country, than the whole race of politicians put together' (p. 176). In Balnibarbi this precept is demonstrated satirically by showing a land where the *reverse* is happening.

    Swift is hitting at what he considered to be abuses of Reason. The Laputans are of course comic creations, caricatures of absent-minded professors, so concerned with the movements of comets that they cannot see what is under their noses. But the comedy has its darker side. The erratic progress of their flying island can cause havoc among the people below, and the wild schemes of their disciples at the Academy are sweeping away the solid achievements of tradition and good craftsmanship. That Swift is attacking the Royal Society is clear: he parodies the style of scientific papers in his account of the magnetic propulsion of Laputa, and many of the lunatic schemes described in Chapter 5 are known to be based on actual scientific papers of the day. But the Academy of Projectors stands for all those institutions which interfere disastrously in matters best left alone. Swift is really stating the classic conservative case, and his Academy also represents the new bureaucratic class – the civil service – which was growing rapidly under Walpole's administration. At the same time he is attacking the new fashion for speculative financial ventures which marked the period. A famous instance is the 'South Sea Bubble', which burst in 1720, ruining many investors, and the reputations of politicians and economists. Yet the heart of the Part is radical enough. The end of Chapter 3 is a thinly disguised warning to Walpole that there is a limit to what the people will endure, and that the penalty for bad government is the overthrow of that government.

The excursions to Glubbdubdrib and to Luggnagg are used to puncture two of mankind's illusions. Gulliver's conversations with great spirits of the past are especially directed against those people in the eighteenth century who liked to think that their age was an improvement on classical antiquity, but anyone who believes in 'progress' is Swift's target here. The other illusion is that a perfect world would be within our grasp if only we were immortal. Thomas Hobbes (1588–1679), the philosopher and author of *Leviathan* (1651) described life as 'nasty, brutish and short'. The parable of the Struldbruggs shows that human beings who lived for ever would only make it nastier, more brutish and eternal. By and large Swift seems to have felt that when the world changes it is usually for the worse. So the third voyage is in some ways the grimmest of the four. The political satire is as severe as anywhere. Despite the high comedy of the Academy of Projectors, much of the humour is grotesque, even surrealist. There is an atmosphere of decay and death and dereliction throughout the journey. In the development of the 'plot' which some find in *Gulliver's Travels* as a whole, this plays an important part. Gulliver returns home armed 'against the fear of death' but with little else to encourage him. When he reappears in Part IV he is prepared to expect the worst. No wonder he finds in the Houyhnhnms a vision of perfection. And no wonder he leaves his **Utopia** with such terrible reluctance.

HOUYHNHNMLAND: THE THEME OF REASON

For his final Part Swift has reserved a surprise change of method. Having looked at man from various angles and in various conditions Gulliver now finds himself faced with the greatest shock of all. In effect Swift has divided man into his two halves, the intellect and the instincts (leaving the soul to shift for itself), and the instincts appear in human shape while the intellect is embodied in that beautiful and odorous quadruped, the horse, whose real superiority to all other beings (for a writer preoccupied with excrement) is symbolised in their superhuman ability to produce pleasantly scented anal products.

The theme of Part IV is, again, Reason. Oddly, however, this is the least intellectual of the Parts, since in a world of Reason there can be no disputation (or so we are told). Instead, much of the Part is taken up with a review of earlier themes. Gulliver explains to his 'master' mankind's methods of settling disputes, war and the law (Chapter 5), and follows his account of politicians and the nobility (Chapter 6) with a fierce critique of the vices of the rich and the parasitical profession of medicine. Medicine, of course, is Gulliver's own profession, so he convicts himself in Chapter 6. But if the themes are largely unchanged, the treatment is markedly different. In Lilliput Gulliver was the innocent observer of wickedness. In Brobdingnag he was its apologist, called upon to defend humanity. In Glubbdubdrib he makes enquiries about human history and his summary is of course a synopsis of Swift's satirical argument. But in Houyhnhnmland Gulliver is under the spell of truth, and his speech amounts to a shrill and guilt-ridden renunciation of humanity and all its works.

By Chapter 8, of course, Gulliver sees man as a Yahoo. So do the Yahoos. And so do the Houyhnhnms. So the verdict appears to be unanimous. But where does Swift stand, and what are we to think? There is no single answer to that question, the Part is far too skilfully constructed to allow one really to *prove* any line of argument. For instance, are the Houyhnhnms an ideal society or not? Certainly they have the best ordered society in *Gulliver's Travels* (even Brobdingnag has beggars). For this the explanation is simple enough:

> As these noble Houyhnhnms are endowed by Nature with a general disposition to all virtues, and have no conceptions or ideas of what is evil in a rational creature, so their grand maxim is to cultivate *Reason*, and to be wholly governed by it. Neither is *Reason* among them a point problematical as with us. (p. 315)

So their perfection is hardly surprising. Their 'cardinal virtues' are friendship and benevolence, which they extend to the whole race (their own race, anyway). Their life is simple but hardy, recalling the virtues of Sparta more than of Athens in the value they put on 'strength, speed and hardiness'. Because they are guided by Reason rather than by appetites their life is without conflict. They face death with stoic calm. In all these ways the Houyhnhnms embody the kind of virtues represented by Swift's own heroes, that 'sextumvirate to which all the ages of the world cannot add a seventh' (p. 241).

And yet the reader may feel that such a life without affection, without humour, without doubt or argument or passion, without any of the circumstances which test our humanity and in fact distinguish the members of that 'sextumvirate' for courage, integrity and stoicism, could have had very little appeal indeed for Swift. Could he have endured those solemn conversations, or those sober poetry recitals? Could he really commend a culture with no books and no history? More important, perhaps, though less likely to occur to us, is the thought that the Houyhnhnms are without religion. As a sincere Christian Swift believed in the revealed truths of his religion, truths which cannot be arrived at by Reason alone, not because they are unreasonable but because they are *beyond* Reason. Reason may be sufficient for a rational creature, but not for a creature with an immortal soul and a capacity for sin.

So is man a Yahoo? The only person in Part IV who does not think so is, ironically, Gulliver's master. Alone of the Houyhnhnms he is willing to think that Gulliver's share of reason was 'in a degree as far inferior to the Houyhnhnm race as the Yahoos of their country were to me'. Read backwards, that is a clear enough sign of Gulliver's true position, neither Houyhnhnm nor Yahoo, but halfway between them, or as Alexander Pope put it in 'An Essay on Man': 'In doubt to deem himself a god, or beast'. This is also true of the narrative effect, for by the end of Part IV Gulliver is thoroughly devoted to the Houyhnhnms, but 'a real Yahoo in every limb and feature'.

Perhaps we have been brought to face a truth about ourselves by being caught up in a remarkable deception. For in this parable about the nature of man, there are no men to be seen, except Gulliver. A neighing, trotting Gulliver, who believes he is a Yahoo, and looks on his wife and children as Yahoos, and yet makes himself a canoe out of Yahoo skins, and who comes to dismiss the entire human race as incapable of amendment, is hardly the best guide to the meaning of a book which, Swift said, 'will wonderfully mend the world'.

There is, however, one man in Part IV, though not in Houyhnhnmland. His name is Don Pedro and he is the closest thing in all Swift's writings to an unqualified portrait of honour, courtesy, friendship and generosity. For some readers, Don Pedro's conduct towards Gulliver, who treats him as a Yahoo, goes beyond anything a Houyhnhnm could understand. For to the Houyhnhnm virtue of benevolence he adds compassion. Liberal readings of Part IV place much stress on the novelistic aspect of the final chapter, arguing that from the moment when Gulliver is forcibly rescued by Don Pedro's crew he discredits himself utterly. After three years of Houyhnhnm tuition, he seems to have lost the ability to draw a rational conclusion from the simplest evidence. Like the animals in Orwell's *Animal Farm* (1945) his whole wisdom seems to be expressible in the slogan 'four legs good, two legs bad'. Of course he tells us the truth about his treatment on this voyage, for he could not 'say the thing that is not', but his own churlish behaviour is quite unaffected by the 'great humanity' of the sailors. While Gulliver enjoys the captain's 'excellent wine' he refuses to borrow 'the best suit of clothes he had' since he could not endure wearing 'any thing that had been on the back of a Yahoo'. Gulliver, it seems, syllogises thus (since he has no reason to suspect Don Pedro of lacking in any decent moral quality): Yahoos have two legs; humans have two legs; therefore humans are Yahoos.

THE VOICE OF SWIFT?

Only a reader who has skipped much of the book will fail to smile when Gulliver claims in Chapter 12 to have written without 'passion, prejudice or ill-will against any man or number of men whatsoever' (p. 342). A little later, despite despising all Yahoos, Gulliver seems to have a few 'scruples' about enlarging his Majesty's dominions by colonisation. At this point, Swift suddenly steps in to raise the argument on to a moral plane which is beyond Gulliver's range. Perhaps we are hearing Swift himself for the first time in the book, in this diatribe against colonial arrogance and butchery, the savagery committed in the name of 'divine right', and the cultural arrogance of 'Christian' conquistadors. From Swift's moral passion, however, we return to the comic and discredited Gulliver, who hopes to reconcile himself to mankind by the absurd remedy of beholding 'my figure often in a glass' (p. 345), and who speaks with unconscious irony, considering how extraordinarily well he recently adapted himself to horse behaviour, of how difficult it is for a man late in life to change 'old habits' (p. 345). Next we hear a more tolerant Gulliver who can accept the sight of 'a lawyer, a pickpocket, a colonel, a fool, a lord, a gamester, a politician, a whoremonger, a physician, an evidence, a suborner, an attorney, a traitor, or the like' since these are 'all according to the due course of things' (p. 345). Surely none of us could be *quite* so tolerant? Certainly not Swift. But Gulliver merges with Swift, briefly, as the sentence continues: 'but when I behold a lump of deformity and diseases both in body and mind, smitten with *pride*, it immediately breaks all the measures of my patience'. At last Gulliver has discovered the unifying theme of all his experiences, and has hit the nail firmly on the head. Yet he falls into the very sin he deplores in his last sentence of all: 'I here entreat those who have any tincture of this absurd vice, that they will not presume to come in my sight' (p. 346). Swift knew as well as anyone that an ironic turn of mind can lead to misanthropy. Perhaps that is why, at the end of the *Travels*, he subjects his hero to burlesque. Vanity, misanthropy and pride are all compounded in Gulliver's final posture: Swift – as construed by many readers of the 'soft' school of interpretation – stands back from this self-portrait, and laughs.

PART FOUR

TEXTUAL ANALYSIS

TEXT 1 A VOYAGE TO LILLIPUT, CHAPTER 2 (PAGES 67–8)

In the meantime, the Emperor held frequent councils to debate what course should be taken with me; and I was afterwards assured by a particular friend, a person of great quality, who was as much in the *secret* as any, that the Court was under many difficulties concerning me. They apprehended my breaking loose, that my diet would be very expensive, and might cause a famine. Sometimes they determined to starve me, or at least to shoot me in the face and hands with poisoned arrows, which would soon dispatch me: but again they considered, that the stench of so large a carcass might produce a plague in the metropolis, and probably spread through the whole kingdom. In the midst of these consultations, several officers of the army went to the door of the great council-chamber; and two of them being admitted, gave an account of my behaviour to the six criminals above-mentioned, which made so favourable an impression in the breast of his Majesty and the whole Board in my behalf, that an Imperial Commission was issued out, obliging all the villages nine hundred yards round the city, to deliver in every morning six beeves [oxen], forty sheep, and other victuals for my sustenance; together with a proportionable quantity of bread, and wine, and other liquors: for the due payment of which, his Majesty gave assignments upon his Treasury. For this Prince lives chiefly upon his own demesnes, seldom except upon great occasions raising any subsidies upon his subjects, who are bound to attend him in his wars at their own expense. An establishment was also made of six hundred persons to be my domestics, who had board-wages allowed for their maintenance, and tents built for them very conveniently on each side of my door. It was likewise ordered, that three hundred tailors should make me a suit of clothes after the fashion of the country: that six of his Majesty's greatest scholars should be employed to instruct me in their language: and, lastly, that the Emperor's horses, and those of the nobility and troops of guards, should be exercised in my sight, to accustom themselves to me. All these orders were duly put in execution, and in about three weeks I made a great progress in learning their language; during which time, the Emperor frequently honoured me with his visits, and was pleased to assist my masters in teaching me. We began already to converse together in some sort; and the first words I learnt were to express my desire that he would please to give me my liberty, which I every day repeated on my knees. His answer, as I could apprehend, was, that this must be a work of time, not to be thought on without the advice of his Council, and that first I must *lumos kelmin pesso desmar lon emposo*; that is, swear a peace with him and his kingdom. However, that I should be used with all kindness, and he advised me to acquire by my patience, and discreet behaviour, the good opinion of himself and his subjects. He desired I would not take it ill, if he gave orders to certain proper officers to search me; for probably I might carry about me several weapons, which must needs be dangerous things, if they answered the bulk of so prodigious a person.

The passage extracted here leads into one of the most successfully comic passages in the text: the inventory of the contents of Gulliver's pockets. Compared with the chapters that follow, this one might seem innocent of satirical intent, but it is subtly infused with satire, sometimes at Gulliver's expense, sometimes against the Lilliputians. We have already seen, in the previous chapter, how Gulliver, bound by 'slender ligatures' to the ground while he is fed, considers himself 'bound by the laws of hospitality' to these tiny creatures for the 'expense and magnificence' of their welcome. He has also identified sufficiently with his captors to describe his ludicrous form of conveyance to the capital as a triumph of mathematics and to speak of how 'we' made a long march. His narrative in this passage is marked by his desire to be thought well of, and the pride he takes in having as a particular friend, 'a person of great quality, who was as much in the secret' as any. This touch invites us to be aware that while Gulliver appears to be in a strange and alien place, in reality he is very much at home, and knows that to survive he must have the best possible intelligence of court intrigue, the most important decisions being taken in secret. The whole matter will be treated far more darkly in Chapter 7.

At this stage, the constant emphasis on numbers probably occupies much of our reading attention. What is meaningful and what isn't? Assuming that his bulk is equivalent to 1728 Lilliputians (a number pretty close to the date of publication) we are probably wondering whether his physical needs are generously or parsimoniously served by six oxen and forty sheep, six hundred domestics, three hundred tailors and six scholars. The result of such analysis is unlikely to get us far: except that the most absurd of these figures is in fact 'six': why would teaching the Man-Mountain require six great scholars; wouldn't one elementary language teacher do just as well? The question whether language is at all subject to scale leads gently into the more important question of the broader moral significance of changes of scale elsewhere in the book. A little later we may be inclined to laugh at the strange inability of the Lilliputians to recognise a hat just because it is six feet high. Are we right or wrong to be amused by Gulliver's apparent awe at the 'majestic deportment' of an Emperor he can hold in his hand? A simple change of scale can change physical reality, but what does it do to moral reality? Have *we* recognised, yet, the real moral nastiness of the court we have been shown?

The question of how Gulliver should be executed is discussed, it seems, wholly in terms of its practicality, not at all in terms of whether he deserves it, and the liberality, if such it is, becomes a matter of political expediency. Was it, in fact, his clemency to the six criminals that made a favourable impression 'in the breast of his Majesty' or his potential as an enforcer of his Majesty's designs? We find out later what Lilliputian clemency means, when the liberal faction at court argue that Gulliver should not be slain (for the treasonable act of putting out a fire under cover of extinguishing a fire) but merely blinded. Are the six scholars there to keep an eye on each other, and the Emperor there to keep an eye on them? As will become clearer in subsequent chapters, Gulliver, at this stage hopelessly naive, and easily flattered into compliance, is in much the same plight as his friends Oxford and Bolingbroke, under investigation by Walpole's administration. So the amusing investigation of his pockets (for signs of treasonable intent) introduces very gently the constant theme of surveillance. This will lead eventually to his impeachment and flight to Blefuscu. In such a climate of suspicion, we may ask for whose convenience does Gulliver have an encampment of six hundred domestics at his door? Gulliver appears not to ask.

Nor does he give any obvious hint whether the Emperor in commandeering so much livestock, from so many villages, in exchange for 'assignments on his treasury' is, in real terms, paying at all. The most obvious political statement in this passage is Gulliver's ambivalent remark that 'this Prince lives chiefly upon his own demesnes, seldom except

TEXT 1 continued

upon great occasions raising any subsidies upon his subjects, who are bound to attend him in his wars at their own expense'. The sentence is a reading instruction, but not yet a clear one. The word 'demesnes' may hint at the perspective of an Anglo-Irish writer aware of the wealth drawn from the peasantry by the owners of great estates. 'His wars' hints strongly at one of the book's recurrent themes, that monarchs make war in their own interests and at their subjects' expense. It may also hint, however, that this monarch depends upon an unpaid militia, and is therefore less arbitrary than a monarch with a standing army. We are being quietly invited to watch, listen and wait. We might attend, for instance to the curious requirement of his majesty that 'the Emperor's horses, and those of the nobility and troops of guards, should be exercised in my sight, to accustom themselves to me', and to the notion that Gulliver's release will be conditional upon swearing 'a peace with him and his kingdom'. Peace with his kingdom can only mean war with someone else's, and the fact that while Gulliver is learning the language the entire national cavalry is being trained to exercise alongside him means that those who have argued for his life see him as a warlike commodity.

TEXT 2   A VOYAGE TO BROBDINGNAG, CHAPTER 7
(PAGES 174–5)

To confirm what I have now said, and further to show the miserable effects of a *confined education*, I shall here insert a passage which will hardly obtain belief. In hopes to ingratiate myself farther into his Majesty's favour, I told him of an invention discovered between three and four hundred years ago, to make a certain powder, into an heap of which the smallest spark of fire falling, would kindle the whole in a moment, although it were as big as a mountain, and make it all fly up in the air together, with a noise and agitation greater than thunder. That, a proper quantity of this powder rammed into an hollow tube of brass or iron, according to its bigness, would drive a ball of iron or lead with such violence and speed as nothing was able to sustain its force. That the largest balls thus discharged, would not only destroy whole ranks of an army at once, but batter the strongest walls to the ground, sink down ships with a thousand men in each, to the bottom of the sea; and when linked together by a chain, would cut through masts and rigging, divide hundreds of bodies in the middle, and lay all waste before them. That we often put this powder into large hollow balls of iron, and discharged them by an engine into some city we were besieging, which would rip up the pavements, tear the houses to pieces, burst and throw splinters on every side, dashing out the brains of all who came near. That I knew the ingredients very well, which were cheap, and common; I understood the manner of compounding them, and could direct his workmen how to make those tubes of a size proportionable to all other things in his Majesty's kingdom, and the largest need not be above two hundred foot long; twenty or thirty of which tubes, charged with the proper quantity of powder and balls, would batter down the walls of the strongest town in his dominions in a few hours, or destroy the whole metropolis, if ever it should pretend to dispute his absolute commands. This I humbly offered to his Majesty as a small tribute of acknowledgement in return of so many marks that I had received of his royal favour and protection.

The King was struck with horror at the description I had given of those terrible engines, and the proposal I had made. He was amazed how so impotent and grovelling an insect as I (these were his expressions) could entertain such inhuman ideas, and in so familiar a manner as to appear wholly unmoved at all the scenes of blood and desolation, which I had painted as the common effects of those destructive machines, whereof he said, some evil genius, enemy to mankind, must have been the first contriver. As for himself, he protested, that although few things delighted him so much as new discoveries in art or in nature, yet he would rather lose half his kingdom than be privy to such a secret, which he commanded me, as I valued my life, never to mention any more.

A strange effect of *narrow principles* and *short views*! that a Prince possessed of every quality which procures veneration, love, and esteem; of strong parts, great wisdom and profound learning, endued with admirable talents for government, and almost adored by his subjects, should from a *nice unnecessary scruple*, whereof in Europe we can have no conception, let slip an opportunity put into his hands, that would have made him absolute master of the lives, the liberties, and the fortunes of his people. Neither do I say this with the least intention to detract from the many virtues of that excellent King, whose character I am sensible will on this account be very much lessened in the opinion of an English reader …

As Gulliver has already informed us, rather patronisingly, great allowances must be made for a king who lives 'wholly secluded from the rest of the world'. The attitudes show 'a certain narrowness of thinking, from which we and the politer countries of Europe are wholly exempted'. Gulliver's judgement is no doubt soured by the king's conclusion in the previous chapter that 'the bulk of your natives' are 'the most pernicious race of little odious vermin that Nature ever suffered to crawl upon the face of the earth'. In any case, applied as the term is to 'notions of virtue and vice', Swift is perhaps warning the reader that 'narrow' may mean correct. Gulliver, however, acts in such a way as to confirm the king in those views. Always willing to flatter and to please, here he miscalculates badly, and confirms by his actions our perniciousness and odiousness. Earlier in Part II he has expressed fear for his life, based on the illogical assumption (he has a very short memory it seems) that creatures are always the more ferocious in proportion to their size: here he seems quite unaware of how his shrunken scale intensifies his own nastiness. He is morally Lilliputian.

The **ironic** technique used here is very simple. Gulliver, who has for much of the time to date represented an innocent eye and ordinary decencies, now represents worldliness. He speaks proudly of the invention of gunpowder, assuming that the king will be grateful. The king, however, is no monstrous potentate. He represents decency, and a 'narrow' sense of scruples. His massive innocence is the scale by which we measure Gulliver's (and our) corruption. The basic technique is intensified by a conspicuous feature of the language in this passage. It is clear that Brobdingnag has no vocabulary for weapons of mass destruction, because it has no concept of such things. The technique of estrangement used in the Man-Mountain's inventory (Part I, Chapter 2) is used again, here, but to entirely different effect.

We see Gulliver himself adopt a **tone** of intrigue, confident of ingratiating himself with the monarch by making him the absolute master of his people. As he describes what gunpowder, cannonballs, chain-shot and siege engines can do, his excitement is expressed in the parallel sentence structures: each sentence continues the grammar of the previous one, eliding the implied '[I told him]' to get on to the next 'that'. The sequence of sentences escalates the scale of violence but also communicates the speaker's attitude, which is somewhere between indifference to human suffering and actual lust for violence. So blind is Gulliver to the impression of moral iniquity that he has already made on this simple decent monarch, that he signals his own involvement by speaking of how 'we' often dash out people's brains and how 'I' can help you reduce your whole capital to ruins. What is our position as readers here? We anticipate the king's response, of course: we predict that he will be horrified rather than gratified at such inhumane proposals. But recognising the irony does not quite allow us to escape. After all, we cannot deny that the callousness which can 'entertain such inhuman ideas', and speak familiarly of 'scenes of blood and desolation' is all too human. Gulliver's naive relish may embarrass us, but unless we regard ourselves as above humanity, we really have nobody else to identify with. We might like to be Brobdingnagian; but we are not.

Gulliver, in any case, entertains no doubts on the matter. He involves us by turning to the reader, confident that we will share his judgement on the king's 'nice unnecessary scruples' and certain that the monarch's character will now be lessened in the eyes of any *English* reader. It is not of course, but somehow the passage has made such simple decency seem more **Utopian**, in the sense that it is far from possible. Gulliver may be amused at the narrowness of a monarch who (as he says in the next paragraph) thinks that 'whoever could make two ears of corn, or two blades of grass, to grow upon a spot of ground where only one grew before, would deserve better of mankind, and do more essential service to this country, than the whole race of politicians together'. We are not amused: it all makes perfect sense. But the fact that this point of view belongs to a monarch 1728 times more *capacious* than ourselves has the curious effect of making us feel that however much we want to believe in such simple and harmonious ideals, it may all be a little beyond our grasp.

In Lilliput, Gulliver only seemed to be an Englishman in a strange place; he was 'really' an innocent foreigner at large in the England of Queen Anne. Here, Gulliver embodies the corruptions of the English constitution and the savagery of European history. Chapter 7 as a whole is one of Swift's clearest statements of a positive political ideal. The hint at the end of this chapter that Brobdingnag has known its own political disorder makes it all the clearer that the stability and simplicity of the Brobdingnagian state is meant as a model for England to imitate.

TEXT 2 continued

Gulliver, our representative, has shrunk morally to a Lilliputian degree of nastiness.

TEXT 3   A VOYAGE TO HOUYHNHNMS, CHAPTER 10 (PAGES 324–5)

I had settled my little economy to my own heart's content. My master had ordered a room to be made for me after their manner, about six yards from the house, the sides and doors of which I plastered with clay, and covered with rush mats of my own contriving; I had beaten hemp, which there grows wild, and made of it a sort of ticking: this I filled with the feathers of several birds I had taken with springes made of Yahoos' hairs, and were excellent food. I had worked two chairs with my knife, the sorrel nag helping me in the grosser and more laborious part. When my clothes were worn to rags, I made myself others with the skins of rabbits, and of a certain beautiful animal about the same size, called *nnuhnoh*, the skin of which is covered with a fine down. Of these I likewise made very tolerable stockings. I soled my shoes with wood which I cut from a tree, and fitted to the upper leather, and when this was worn out, I supplied it with the skins of Yahoos dried in the sun. I often got honey out of hollow trees, which I mingled with water, or ate it with my bread. No man could more verify the truth of these two maxims, *That nature is very easily satisfied*; and, *That necessity is the mother of invention*. I enjoyed perfect health of body and tranquillity of mind; I did not feel the treachery or inconstancy of a friend, nor the injuries of a secret or open enemy. I had no occasion of bribing, flattering or pimping, to procure the favour of any great man or of his minion. I wanted no fence against fraud or oppression; here was neither physician to destroy my body, nor lawyer to ruin my fortune; no informer to watch my words and actions, or forge accusations against me for hire: here were no gibers, censurers, backbiters, pickpockets, highwaymen, housebreakers, attorneys, bawds, buffoons, gamesters, politicians, wits, splenetics, tedious talkers, controvertists, ravishers, murderers, robbers, virtuosos; no leaders or followers of party and faction; no encouragers to vice, by seducement or examples: no dungeon, axes, gibbets, whippingposts, or pillories; no cheating shopkeepers or mechanics: no pride, vanity, or affectation: no fops, bullies, drunkards, strolling whores, or poxes: no ranting, lewd, expensive wives: no stupid, proud pendants [pedants, as in other editions, seems more likely]: no importunate, overbearing, quarrelsome, noisy, roaring, empty, conceited, swearing companions: no scoundrels, raised from the dust upon the merit of their vices, or nobility thrown into it on account of their virtues: no Lords, fiddlers, Judges or dancing-masters.

The opening style of this paragraph appears nowhere else in the book. The style is so lyrical, as Gulliver describes his contentedness among the Houyhnhnms, or rather as an isolated figure in their land, that we might suspect Swift of contriving it for several purposes. One purpose, of course, is to increase Gulliver's tragic sense of expulsion, when he learns that he is sentenced to leave his equine paradise. The headnote ensures that dramatic irony operates in our reading of the passage: we already know, as Gulliver does not, that he will not be allowed to stay. Another purpose is to draw attention to his Robinson Crusoe-like isolation: what real intimacy is possible to Gulliver among a 'people' who are not people, whose language has no way of expressing doubt, whose literature is the epitome of blandness, and so on? He mentions no society in this paragraph, and what follows merely emphasises the implied isolation. The next paragraph tells us how Gulliver is favoured by 'admission' to houses, where the company 'descend' to ask him questions, and his station is that of 'an humble auditor'. Where there is no equality, Adam said, when asking God to make him a female companion, there is no society.

The treatment of Gulliver's contentment is notable for two things. First, his 'tranquillity of mind' is defined almost entirely by negatives. When he has described himself as housed, fed, clothed, and shod, he has exhausted the positives. Tranquillity is glossed very beautifully as consisting in this: 'I did not feel the treachery and inconstancy of a friend, nor the injuries of a secret or open enemy'. This sentence has all the characteristic poise of **Augustan** composition. It is so beautifully balanced between treachery and inconstancy, secret and open, friend and enemy, that we hardly notice how it redefines friend and enemy as a distinction without real difference. What tranquillity is this? The vacuum of undefined content is rapidly filled by one of the book's most one-sided expressions of misanthropy. The long sentence is a sort of prose poem, beautifully elegiac in its rhythms. Read it aloud to notice how the units of the sentence are both parallel and varied. First, in 'neither physician … nor lawyer' he despatches the two professions he most likes to hate (they are attacked throughout the *Travels*). Next he defines a single profession (of informer) by two actions. Next comes a catalogue of some twenty 'occupations' incorporating such libellous associations of ideas as 'attorneys, bawds, buffoons', followed, for variety, by a short parallelism ('no leaders or followers of party and faction'). Standing out from the whole sentence are the brief glint of misogyny, 'no ranting, lewd, expensive wives' (which compresses woman's three vices into one summative indictment); the summary of the relative political rewards of vice and virtue; and the final contemptuous 'no Lords, fiddlers, Judges or dancing-masters' where the *apparent* randomness belies an implied equation of Lords to those who fiddle, and Judges to those who reward 'dancers', like the leapers and crawlers of Lilliput.

Relishing such a sentence with its skilful **anaphora**, brings out one of the great paradoxes about *Gulliver's Travels*. Some of its most pessimistic denigrations of humanity combine Swift's libels on the species with an exhibition of marvellous, life-enhancing, art. 'God, that's horrible!' and 'God, that's beautiful!' can be simultaneous reactions. This compound reaction can incur a kind of guilt in the reader: ought aesthetic pleasure to accompany moral shock?

The instability of Gulliver's present stage of contentment may be implied in the two maxims he offers. These may be intended to satirise human kind's perennial yearning for the simple life, based on the notion that *our* 'nature is very easily satisfied', by pointing out that to homo sapiens, homo faber, or whatever other definition of man you adopt, 'necessity is the mother of invention'. The gap between these two maxims may point to the impossibility of a Houyhnhnm existence to creatures constituted as we are. Moreover, as you may have noticed, the simple diction of the passage, dealing with building a simple home of clay and rushes (it is hard not to think of William Butler Yeats's much later poem, 'The Lake Isle of Innisfree') conceals an underlying horror. If Gulliver does recognise himself as a Yahoo, what is he doing not merely making 'springes' [snares] out of Yahoo hairs, but shoes out of sun-dried Yahoo skin? Part IV has been read as a particularly ferocious part of Swift's assault on colonialism and on the kind of ideology (the alleged cannibalism of savages) used to justify it. So the simple paradox built into the two maxims can be read as pointing to a broader political point, to do with the white man's ruination and exploitation of native peoples who get in his way. Who is the cannibal?

Shortly after this paragraph, Gulliver reaches his most tragic conclusion about the species: 'When I thought of my family, my friends, my countrymen, or human race in general, I considered them as they really were, Yahoos in shape and disposition, perhaps a little more civilized, and qualified with the gift of speech, but making no other use of Reason, than to improve and multiply those vices, whereof their brethren in this country had only the share that Nature allotted them'. This conclusion, which may of course be wrong even if Gulliver, the Yahoos and Houyhnhnms all think it is right, leads immediately to a tragic and very understandable sense of self-loathing: 'When I happened to behold the reflection of my own form in a lake or a fountain, I turned away my face in horror and detestation of myself, and could better endure the sight of a common Yahoo, than of my own person'. Yet the note changes immediately from tragic to comic: 'By conversing with the Houyhnhnms, and looking upon them with delight, I fell to imitate their gait and gesture, which is now grown into a habit, and my friends often tell me in a blunt way, that I trot like a horse; which, however, I take for a great compliment: neither shall I disown, that in speaking I am apt to fall into the voice and manner of the Houyhnhnms, and hear myself ridiculed on that account without the least mortification'. Those three consecutive sentences summarise very well the quandary Part IV is designed to place us in: does this book express a tragic sense of life, or ridicule a Gulliver who got it all comically wrong?

PART FIVE

BACKGROUND

JONATHAN SWIFT

Swift was born on 30 November 1667 in Dublin. His father having died before Jonathan's birth, an uncle, Godwin Swift, saw to it that his nephew received a good education, first at Kilkenny School and then at Trinity College, Dublin, from which he graduated in 1686. The family was an English one which had settled in Ireland shortly after the death of Swift's grandfather, Thomas Swift, a clergyman who had been removed from his church in Herefordshire during the Cromwellian period to be replaced by a Dissenting minister.

When political and civil strife broke out in Ireland after the Glorious Revolution of 1688 it was natural that Swift was among those who returned to England, where in 1689 family influence obtained for him the post of private secretary to Sir William Temple. Temple was a distinguished diplomat, retired, a leading liberal, and a man of culture and intelligence. In his house, Moor Park in Surrey, Swift not only enjoyed a life of elegance and stimulating companionship, but also became known to Temple's powerful friends in aristocratic and political circles.

Severe illness caused Swift to return to Ireland in the summer of 1690. He had experienced his first attack of Ménière's disease – an illness which attacks the inner ear, causing giddiness, vomiting and deafness. This recurred with increasing intensity throughout his life. This disease was not medically recognised until 1861: its effects on a man of Swift's energies and temperament helped to create the legend of Swift the misanthrope and the madman, especially as it seemed such a convenient explanation of the savage force of his satirical writings. In 1690 all his doctors could advise was a change of climate. But finding no work in Ireland he was soon back at Moor Park. Here he developed his own literary powers, with access to Sir William's fine library, and found himself involved in political affairs. In 1694, offended by the offer of an obscure appointment, he angered Temple by returning to Dublin. By the spring of 1695 he was installed in the parish of Kilroot, near Belfast. But

Kilroot could in no way compensate for Moor Park, so by May 1696 he was back for his third stay with Temple. Although when Temple died in 1699 Swift was still without a living, he had composed three of his most famous satires, *A Tale of a Tub*, *The Battle of the Books*, and the *Discourse Concerning the Mechanical Operation of the Spirit*.

Now thirty-two, Swift returned to Ireland as chaplain to the Earl of Berkeley, one of the Irish Lords Justice, and in the following year, 1700, became Vicar of Laracor, a parish north of Dublin in County Meath. Swift was no less conscientious than the average churchman of the time but did not allow his work there to interrupt his political concerns. In 1701 he was in London again, and wrote a pamphlet praising the conduct of the Whig, or liberal, leaders. This work, *A Discourse of the Contests and Dissensions between the Nobles and the Commons in Athens and Rome*, made his reputation and he was soon known as the author of several pamphlets in the Whig interest as well as of *A Tale of a Tub* and *The Battle of the Books*, written at Moor Park but published only in 1704.

Swift's intellectual upbringing had been thoroughly Whig, both in Temple's service and later in Berkeley's. In parliament the first minister, Sidney Godolphin (1645–1712), was himself a Tory, but served as Lord Treasurer of predominantly Whig governments from 1702 to 1710. During this period Swift formed friendships with members of the Godolphin ministry and with the writers Steele and Addison, and he expected that the services he performed for the Whigs with his acid pen would be rewarded by promotion to an English bishopric. In the years 1708–9 he wrote a series of deeply felt religious pamphlets, such as *Sentiments of a Church of England Man* and the ironic *Argument against Abolishing Christianity*. While aiding the Whigs, his deepest concern was the defence of Church interests, and by the end of the decade he found that the Whigs were likely to pass legislation damaging to the Church.

Swift was about to make a dramatic political about turn. He had been campaigning for a measure known as 'Remission of the First Fruits' to be extended to the Irish Church (the 'first fruits' system meant that a new minister of the Church had to pay his first year's income to a superior, and it had been reformed in England but not in Ireland). The Whigs would only allow this as part of a deal including the repeal of the Test Act, which denied political office to non-Anglicans. In Swift's eyes this was too high a price to pay, for he feared the political tendencies of religious enthusiasts whether Catholic or Dissenters. The Tory leaders Harley and St John thought Swift's pen worth having on their side, and they bought his services with the legislation he had worked for for so long. Swift used his influence to help his old friends, the essayists Steele and Addison and the dramatist Congreve, but he soon found congenial friendships among the Tories. He became one of the famous 'Scriblerus Club', an association of witty writers which included St John himself, Alexander Pope the famous poet, John Gay the dramatist, and Dr Arbuthnot.

As editor of a Tory journal, *The Examiner*, and author of a brilliant attack on Marlborough and the Whigs called *The Conduct of the Allies*, Swift helped to maintain public support for the Tory ministry. Yet once again his new friends were unable to obtain for him high office in the Church in England. Not even Harley could soften Queen Anne towards the author of *A Tale of a Tub* when her closest friends and advisers, the Duchess of Somerset and the Archbishop of York, had described that work as profane and irreligious; and in fairness to the Queen that criticism of Swift's religious polemic is hard to refute.

In 1714 instead of being appointed to a place in England he returned to Dublin as Dean of St Patrick's Cathedral. Disappointed though he was, the promotion had come just in time. The Tory ministry fell apart. Swift visited London in a vain attempt to reconcile Harley and St John – now known as the Earl of Oxford and Viscount Bolingbroke respectively – but after the Queen's death in that year the Tories fell from power. A year later Bolingbroke was in exile in France, and Oxford was imprisoned in London, both under suspicion of treason. In Bolingbroke's case these suspicions were not groundless: he was on good terms with Jacobite sympathisers (those who wished to restore the Stuart dynasty with French aid). But Swift knew nothing against his friends and he remained loyal to them when to do so was dangerous, even foolhardy. He defended them soberly in his *History of the Last Four Years of the Queen*: but this work of serious contemporary history was not published until 1758. A different kind of defence, however, appeared in *Gulliver's Travels* (1726) in which his friends are combined in the giant form of Gulliver, ~mented by Whiggish pygmies.

In Ireland Swift soon made new friends among the clergy, including Thomas Sheridan and Patrick Delaney. By 1720 he was deeply involved in Irish affairs. In that year the Whigs passed an act to increase the dependency of Ireland on Britain. In reply Swift wrote his *Proposal for the Universal Use of Irish Manufacture*, instructing his fellow-countrymen in the art of economic self-reliance. When the government of Sir Robert Walpole, the new Whig leader, sought to impose a new coinage on Ireland known as Wood's half-pence (because the Londoner William Wood had been granted a licence to mint the coins) Swift responded with his series of Drapier's Letters. These brilliant pieces, under the pseudonym 'M. B. Drapier', culminated in *A Letter to the Whole People of Ireland* (1724) and succeeded in so uniting the Irish – at least the Anglo-Irish elite to which Swift belonged – that the project was dropped. A reward of £300 was offered for proof of the writer's identity but no one in Ireland would now convict Swift. He had become a national hero.

By this time he had started his great work, *Gulliver's Travels*, written in 1721–5. His later writings include the bitter *Short View of the State of Ireland* (1728) and his most brilliant short satire *A Modest Proposal* (1729). Throughout the thirties he was writing fine verse, including the autobiographical *Verses on the Death of Dr Swift* (1731), and in 1736 came a biting attack on the Irish Parliament, *The Legion Club*. His illness had worsened steadily. In 1742 he was declared incapable of managing his own affairs, and he lingered on, in pain and isolation, until his death on 19 October 1745. He was buried in his own cathedral under an epitaph of his own composition, in Latin. We know it best in the version by another great Anglo-Irish writer, W.B. Yeats:

> *Swift has sailed into his rest;*
> *Savage indignation there*
> *Cannot lacerate his breast.*
> *Imitate him if you dare,*
> *World-besotted traveller; he*
> *Served human liberty.*

At his death it was found that Swift, who had in his lifetime given away a third of his modest income, had saved another third which he left for the building of a hospital for the insane. It was a characteristic parting stroke for one who had devoted his wit to exposing the infirmities of the world, to protect from that world those whose wits had proved too infirm to take the strain of existence.

VARINA, STELLA AND VANESSA

The name of this bachelor clergyman has always been associated with three young women who entered his life at various critical points in his career. At Kilroot, the remote parish where he worked in 1695, he proposed marriage to Jane Waring, whom he called 'Varina'. She rejected him at first and Swift's pride was stung. When in 1700 she changed her mind Swift had changed his. He offered marriage once more, but in such cold and insulting terms that he knew she could only reject them. By then, Swift had played his part in the education of Esther Johnson, a girl in Temple's household at Moor Park. The connection was such that 'Stella', as he called her, decided to settle in Ireland after Swift's appointment at Laracor. She became Swift's lifelong friend. Some people believe that they were secretly married. Swift and Stella were in daily contact when he was in Ireland, and he wrote to her an intimate journal throughout his visits to England. Each year he celebrated her birthday in tender, playful verses. He seems to have deliberately kept his relationship with this brilliant younger woman at a playful level, perhaps fearful of its turning into a deeper passion. When she was sick Swift could scarcely bear it. When she died he could not bring himself to attend her funeral, but consoled himself by writing a moving account of her life: 'the truest, most virtuous, and valuable friend that I, or perhaps any other person, ever was blessed with'.

If there was a marriage between them it must have been as secret reassurance to Stella that another of Swift's admirers could never replace her. In London, during his visits on church business in 1707–9, and in the Tory period up to 1714, he had established a friendship with Esther Vanhomrigh, eldest daughter of a brilliant household which was a centre of Anglo-Irish society. 'Vanessa', as he called her, followed Swift to Ireland in 1714 driven by a passion which he could not return, though he had thoughtlessly encouraged her at the start, and which he fended off as gently as possible. The early part of this relationship is described in the poem 'Cadenus and Vanessa', where Cadenus (an **anagram** for *decanus*, Latin for Dean) subjects this unequal relationship to clear scrutiny at his expense more than hers. Vanessa died in 1723 after the affair had passed through many stormy episodes.

SOME OF SWIFT'S OTHER WORKS

A Tale of a Tub, written mostly in 1696 and published anonymously in 1704, made Swift's literary reputation. It makes difficult reading today because it is written in a skilful parody of learned ecclesiastical English. The work offended Queen Anne, and many other readers, since it is easy to see it as a mockery of all religious belief. It was intended as a fable demonstrating that of all the varieties of Christianity available in the eighteenth century the Anglican is the purest, or at least relatively free of corruptions.

The Battle of the Books, published with the *Tale*, is Swift's contribution to a debate started by Sir William Temple as to whether ancient or modern writings were of greater value. In its argument that modern thinkers are guilty of pride in neglecting the wisdom of the past, the *Battle*, though written in an allusive and learned style, is closely related to two sections of Gulliver's third voyage, the attack on modern science in Laputa, and Gulliver's talks with the spirits in Glubbdubdrib.

The first pamphlet Swift wrote in defence of the Whigs was his *Discourse of the Contests and Dissensions in Athens and Rome* (1701). To an Irishman, only two years after William had defeated the Jacobite forces in Ireland, the rising power of the Tories and their willingness to go to extreme lengths to discredit the Whigs were very alarming matters. *The Contests and Dissensions* is a warning to the Tories not to weaken the nation by their partisan activities – though Swift also cautions the Whigs against giving encouragement to Dissenters. It remained well-known, and is cited as authoritative political history by John Adams in his *A Defence of the Constitutions of Government of the United States of America* (1787).

The *Argument against Abolishing Christianity* (1708) is one of a number of religious works written at the time Swift was becoming uneasy about the Whigs. More important, it is also one of his most exuberantly ironical pieces, the first to be written in Swift's wonderful combination of plain English with elaborate flights of irony.

The finest of Swift's achievements as a Tory propagandist was his *The Conduct of the Allies* (1711), which helped to bring about peace by describing the war with France as a national calamity continued for private profit by Marlborough and Godolphin. Fair or not, the pamphlet is persuasive and hard hitting, and provided the Tories with most of their arguments in parliamentary debate. It finished Marlborough's career. Swift's first influential contribution to Irish affairs was *A Proposal for the Universal Use of Irish Manufacture* (1720). Trading arrangements appeared to be fixed with a view to the deliberate ruination of Ireland. Here Swift asserts the right of the Irish to import and export as their own needs required, rather than under legislation designed to protect England's trade at Ireland's expense.

HISTORICAL & LITERARY BACKGROUND

SWIFT AND THE AUGUSTANS

The turmoil of the seventeenth century, before, during, and between the revolutions of 1649 and 1688, seems to have instilled in most writers of Swift's time a love of order, restraint, good sense, and a distrust of religious enthusiasts and political innovators. Writers of the age modelled themselves upon classical rather than gothic models, especially the writers of Rome's Augustan age, Virgil, Horace and Ovid, imitating their regularity of form, clarity and elegance. The literary style of Sir William Temple, the essayists Addison and Steele, the poet Alexander Pope, and the dramatist John Gay is a social one, and, by comparison with the ornate and elaborate productions of seventeenth-century prose, simple and direct. It combines regularity and elegance, with light, clarity and concision, in the verbal equivalent of beautifully proportioned Queen Anne or Georgian architecture.

In the small London society of clubs and coffee houses, the production of literature was in any case a social activity, an activity epitomised in the polite essays of the Whig journalists Joseph Addison and Richard Steele, or Sir William Temple, and equally so in the work of Swift's Tory friends Dr John Arbuthnot, a scientist and the Queen's physician, the comic dramatist John Gay, and the most elegant of poets,

Alexander Pope. John Gay's comedy, *The Beggar's Opera* (1728), on a theme suggested by Swift, is a social satire on the similarity of vice in low and high places, set in Newgate. Pope's poems brought to perfection the wit, balance, and elegance of the heroic couplet, whether in the mock-heroic *The Rape of the Lock*, his demonstration of poetic craftsmanship in *An Essay on Criticism*, the attack on bad taste in *The Dunciad*, or the encapsulation of common sense philosophy in *An Essay on Man*. Swift's friendships with such writers reminds us of his sociability and his membership of a milieu marked by elegance and attachment to what was thought of as good sense. But it does bring out a radical difference between Swift and his friends. In *The Tatler* and *The Spectator*, Addison and Steele's amiable essays encouraged moral reflections on all manner of topics, in an easy familiar style, but steered well clear of contentious issues in politics. Pope might be unfairly represented by his critical demand for poetry to content itself with 'what oft was thought but ne'er so well expressed', but his complacent philosophy is never much more demanding than 'whatever is, is right'. Augustan satire is generally a conservative art, contenting itself with ridicule of whatever fails to meet standards of good taste and good sense. This manicured 'Age of Reason' provoked, at the end of the century, a Romantic revolt in favour of change, diversity, energy, individuality, the natural and the unconscious, both in the aspirations and revolutionary demands of Romantic poetry and in that ultimate interrogation of Reason and order, the Gothic novel. Swift's work is almost alone in the Augustan period in seeming to include the disturbances his contemporaries kept well under control.

SWIFT AND RELIGION

The eighteenth century saw the rise of a sentimental view of man in which it was increasingly assumed that man is naturally good. It was the era of 'The Noble Savage'. Man's conduct is motivated, when social conditions are favourable, by sympathy and benevolence, and as he is naturally rational so he is naturally virtuous. Such ideas appear in the liberal philosophers of Swift's time, and again in William Godwin at the end of the century: they end up as utilitarianism in the Victorian period, and as liberal humanism today. Swift was untouched by such ideas. He took a sternly traditional view of man as a fallen creature, in need of redemption, driven by lust, greed and envy, or almost anything but Reason. The attack on mankind in *Gulliver's Travels* may strike modern readers as too severe for a Christian writer, yet his critique is no more extreme than one might find in seventeenth-century sermons, and a few years after Swift's death the great religious reformer John Wesley (1703–91) found in *Gulliver* admirable proofs for the doctrine of Original Sin.

Unlike Wesley, however, what seems to be missing in Swift is any evidence of religious zeal. As an Anglican he seems to expend more energy mocking religious enthusiasm than encouraging faith. For this the reasons are historical. His grandfather had been persecuted by evangelical Puritans in Cromwell's time, and in Ireland he belonged to a minority faith in a land of Catholics. To any Anglican Tory in Swift's day, dissent was considered synonymous with Cromwell's political tyranny, and Catholics were identified with Jacobite treason. Swift believed sincerely that the tolerant middle-of-the-road Anglican Church, associated with the kind of constitutional monarchy established by the Glorious Revolution of 1688, was the commonsense position. To defend religious liberty for all, it was paradoxically necessary to deny political power to Dissenters or to Catholics who, it was believed, would use such power to deny any liberty at all to people of other persuasions. To understand how natural it seemed in the age of Swift for a churchman to expend most of his energies in political activity it is necessary to look at the historical background, and the events to which *Gulliver's Travels* refers.

COMMONWEALTH AND RESTORATION

In 1629 King Charles I dissolved Parliament. Only when his attempt to impose his own religion on the Scots brought about a Scottish revolution did he summon Parliament again to raise money for an army. Parliament refused to subscribe, and in 1642 Charles fled from London and Parliament prepared for civil war: a war between 'Cavaliers' (Scots Catholics and English Royalists) on the one hand, and 'Roundheads' (Scots Presbyterians and English Protestants) on the other. In the course of the war Oliver Cromwell had trained a Roundhead army of exceptional effectiveness and religious zeal, which was unwilling to disband when Parliament attempted to dismiss it. A second civil war led to the execution of Charles in 1649, and the abolition of the Monarchy and of the House of Lords. For ten years England was ruled by Cromwell as Lord Protector, and by religious Dissenters, or Puritans. But the Commonwealth did not survive Cromwell's death.

In 1660 Charles II was crowned, at the invitation of a newly elected Parliament. At first the transition was achieved peaceably. An Act of Indemnity prevented excessive acts of revenge, and a large body of former Roundheads remained in possession of lands and wealth formerly owned by Royalists. In consequence the Parliament of the early years was made up partly of old Cavaliers, the Tory squires, and partly of old Roundheads. The Tory majority began to exact a different kind of revenge by religious persecution of Dissenters. In the course of time the Roundhead element in Parliament began to gain strength, and the Tory or High Church Party found itself opposed by a Whig Party composed of Puritan sympathisers and progressive free-thinkers who believed in religious toleration, at least for Protestants.

Kept short of money by the Parliament which had restored his crown, and which was aligned with the Dutch in their struggle against France, Charles II looked increasingly towards France and alliance with Louis XIV. He made a public treaty with Louis, who wished to attack and partition Holland, and a private treaty that would enable him to use French money and French soldiers to support his plan to impose Catholicism and absolute monarchy on England. Holland's victory put an end to this plot, and forced Charles to adapt himself to his Anglican Parliament. But Parliament, under Tory High Church dominance, used its new power to crush the Dissenters more vigorously than ever. In their turn the rising Whig party took savage revenge against suspected Catholics. The pendulum swung back and forth, and Parliament was again weakening itself by these factional feuds.

THE GLORIOUS REVOLUTION OF 1688

The first great event of James II's reign was a new Puritan revolt against the Catholic monarch, led by the Duke of Monmouth. Again the King's response was excessive. The flood of executions horrified moderate opinion, and James attempted to secure his power by recruiting an overwhelmingly Catholic army, which he installed near the capital to impress the people. He established a standing army of 30,000 men, and nothing could have alienated his natural supporters, the royalist Tory squires, more than this clumsy reminder of recent tyranny. James, in his policy of emulating Louis, antagonised both the English (including moderate Catholics) and the Pope himself. The English, watching the French persecution of the Protestant Huguenots (who arrived in England in thousands), saw that similar horrors were in store for them.

In 1688 William of Orange landed in Torbay. James's army deserted, and the people united about the new King, William, and his English Queen, Mary. The King was to rule with the consent of Parliament. Religious toleration became established, except that political power was denied to Catholics or Dissenters. A Protestant succession was assured. To most Englishmen, and certainly to Swift, the balance between King, Church, and Parliament, brought about by the so-called Revolution Settlement, was a triumph of common sense. It is certainly the foundation of Swift's political views.

WAR WITH FRANCE

The Revolution succeeded so painlessly because John Churchill, the future Duke of Marlborough, had abandoned James's army at the critical moment, and William's policy of containment of France was to be made possible by this brilliant soldier. War with France was inevitable if William was to ensure the failure of Jacobitism, that is, attempts to restore James and a Catholic monarchy in Britain. Parliament willingly financed the campaign. Marlborough led Protestant Europe throughout the War of the Spanish Succession (1701–13) and won great victories at Blenheim in 1704, and Ramillies in 1706. His victories were achieved by military genius supported by an anti-Jacobite alliance of Whigs and moderate Tories, who controlled the parliamentary purse.

But war is expensive. By 1709 Louis and Marlborough, and most of the English people, were ready for a just peace. Except for occupation of France itself, war could accomplish no more. But the Whigs were after total victory, as war cabinets usually are. At this point a series of domestic disasters caused a change of government (and Swift's change of sides). Queen Anne had succeeded her brother-in-law in 1702: she, and her new

Tory ministry of 1710, desired peace. In 1713 they achieved it by the controversial Treaty of Utrecht. The treaty was deplored by the Whig leaders for its leniency to France, and when the Whigs returned to power in 1714 under the Hanoverian King George I, both Oxford and Bolingbroke were impeached for their role in the secret negotiations that brought it about, negotiations that appeared the more treasonable since the Pretender (James III as he wished to be) was involved. The Whigs were to remain in power throughout the next two reigns, until 1760. For twenty-one of those years the country was governed by Sir Robert Walpole, who came to power in 1721, just as Swift was beginning Part I of *Gulliver's Travels*.

THE SITUATION OF IRELAND

Ever since Pope Adrian IV requested King Henry II to conquer Ireland in 1154 there had been Norman, English or Scottish elements in possession of parts of Ireland. But no monarch ever succeeded in making a real union between the Irish and the other British peoples. About once a century the Irish revolted and were put down by the English, some of whom remained to be absorbed by the Irish and participate in the next rising. The major result of this policy of alternate neglect and punitive raids was that Ireland remained a poor country whose native people were almost wholly Catholic and sympathetic to a whole succession of enemies of England – from Spain in Elizabeth's time to the French in Swift's.

Swift thought of himself as English. At the time of the Battle of the Boyne, when William defeated James II in 1690 (the Glorious Revolution had been peaceful in England but was bloody in Ireland), Swift was with Temple in Surrey. Yet from 1714 onwards he became increasingly known as an Irish patriot. What he experienced in Ireland was very similar to the experience of the American colonists under George III – all the disadvantages of direct rule from London, and none of the advantages. Since no politician in England gave much thought to Ireland, the land was bled by absentee landlords, denied fair trading terms, and ruled by second-rate officials who could behave irresponsibly with no one to care about the consequences. Hardly any of the major posts in Irish administration were filled by native-born Irishmen.

In the face of neglect, decay and outright oppression, Swift became a reluctant patriot, showing how the colonial power might be resisted. There was nothing radical about Swift's social and political views. He believed in order and authority – though less so when authority was Whig. He believed that society is a hierarchy in which Princes owe protection to their subjects, and masters to their servants, while these in turn owe loyalty to their masters and princes. What was radical was that he applied this belief to Ireland. The Anglo-Irish, he felt, had been denied their rights as free men. They were oppressed because they were not enjoying the fair application of the principles of the Revolution Settlement. He felt he was living among a nation of 'beggars, thieves, oppressors, fools and knaves', but scornful though he was towards the Irish and their unwillingness to help themselves, his most savage indignation was reserved for Ireland's absentee government. Walpole's Whig ministry in London was the real target of a stream of pamphlets he produced on Irish matters in the 1720s, the decade of *Gulliver's Travels*.

PART SIX

CRITICAL HISTORY & BROADER PERSPECTIVES

RECEPTION & CONTROVERSY

From the outset, some of Jonathan Swift's readers found the author of *Gulliver's Travels* guilty of a plot to 'depreciate human nature' (Lord Bolingbroke) or of 'a real insult upon mankind' (the Earl of Orrery). The first work of sustained criticism, Orrery's *Remarks on the Life and Writings of Dr Jonathan Swift* (1752) ensured that eighteenth-century debate focused upon supporting or contesting the notion that Swift's work manifested an extreme misanthropy, and was explicable only as the ravings of a deranged and disappointed man. Deane Swift, Swift's cousin, in his *Essay upon the Life, Writings, and Character of Jonathan Swift* (1755) argued that the work, rather than libelling human nature, satirised folly, corruption, pride, political factions and religious intolerance, and should therefore be understood as a defence of human nature when free of such moral blights.

Since the early assault on Swift was strongest among those who believed in the dignity and perfectibility of human nature, it is perhaps surprising that in the nineteenth and twentieth centuries, radical democrats such as William Godwin and William Hazlitt in the Romantic era and Michael Foot (the left wing MP and Hazlitt scholar) in the twentieth century have staunchly defended Swift. However, social satirists or denunciatory prophets, such as Thackeray, the Victorian novelist, and Aldous Huxley and D. H. Lawrence in the 1930s, found themselves at odds with him. Godwin, author of *Political Justice* (1793), found in Gulliver 'a generous indignation against vice, and an ardent love of every thing that is excellent and honourable to the human heart'. William Makepeace Thackeray, however, advised his genteel Victorian readers in 1853 not to read the fourth book, lest they expose themselves to 'a monster gibbering shrieks, and gnashing imprecations against mankind – tearing down all shreds of modesty, past all sense of manliness and shame; filthy in word, filthy in thought, furious, raging, obscene' (*Lectures on the English Humourists*). Which is to say, perhaps, that Swift appeals to social critics in a revolutionary epoch, more than to social critics within a bourgeois frame.

For selections from eighteenth- and nineteenth-century assessments see:

Kathleen Williams, *Swift: the Critical Heritage* (Routledge & Kegan Paul, 1970)

Denis Donoghue, ed., *Jonathan Swift: a Critical Anthology* (Penguin, 1971)

Richard Gravil, ed., *Swift: Gulliver's Travels* (Macmillan, 1974).

MODERN SCHOLARSHIP

Early twentieth-century critics focused first upon recovering the political context of Swift's work, and upon establishing its relatedness to a variety of literary traditions. Sir Charles Firth (1919) and A.E. Case (1945) read *Gulliver* as containing detailed **allegory** of the politics of Queen Anne's court, and the careers of his associates and adversaries. It is clear, however, that Swift's **satire** has a more general application, or his work would have dated as rapidly as that of Dryden. Annotations add an interesting dimension, but *Gulliver's Travels* remains of value as satire precisely because (unlike the obscurer references in many political satires) his barbs communicate meaningfully whether or not we are aware of contemporary references, or of the in-jokes, which his contemporaries could enjoy. Odious little Tories or verminous little Whigs are always with us. Perhaps it helps, too, that critics are hopelessly divided on the nature of Swift's politics. As Ian Higgins in Rawson (1995) summarises the matter: 'For F.P. Lock, Swift is a natural Tory. For J.A. Downie, Swift is an unreconstructed Revolution Whig'.

Since *Gulliver's Travels* is neither a political history nor a novel, critics have regularly sought to find a literary tradition within which to place it, such as narratives of imaginary travels, or visits to ideal commonwealths, designed to mirror society or to anatomise social ethics. Nineteenth-century critics were alert to Swift's **allusions** to a range of work describing real or imaginary travels, earlier parodies of such narratives, social **anatomies Utopias** and **Dystopias**. Jenny Mecziems

(1977) sees this relationship as central to Swift's investigation of the reality or unreality of ideal projections of human life. Marjorie Hope Nicolson and Nora M. Mohler (1956), in a much cited essay, inaugurated a continuing fascination with Swift's grasp of science, showing how much of Laputa was inspired by papers of the Royal Academy and by such disorienting experiences as looking at familiar tissues through a microscope. *Gulliver's Travels* originates from a culture fascinated by experiment, invention, classification, exhibition (Gulliver is himself exhibited and classified in Brobdingnag) and also by the efforts of scientific and economic 'projectors' of all kinds.

Ricardo Quintana's major studies of Swift (1936/53 and 1955), and his excellent 1948 essay 'Situational Satire: A Commentary on the Method of Swift' (*University of Toronto Quarterly 17*), steered critics away from biographical interpretations of Swift's writings, inaugurating a decade of attention to the formal characteristics of Swift's art. One temptation in such forms of analysis is to suppose that Swift's work, if one understands the rules well enough, is ultimately analysable: once you have grasped which of a finite number of satiric techniques is in play, you can feel safely in control of your reading experience. But Claude Rawson (1970), in 'Order and Cruelty', and Robert C. Elliott (1960), in 'Swift's Satire: Rules of the game' (the essays are presented in tandem in Rawson – 1995), explore the way Swift's satire, as Rawson puts it, 'often suggests an impasse, a blocking of escape routes and saving possibilities', so that reader and author seem to be ineluctably implicated in the critique. Moreover, one can feel at one moment a kind of aesthetic joy in the sheer beauty of some of Swift's most horrific assaults, and yet recognise in the next that Swift himself sometimes appears guilt-ridden about the practice of so damaging and hate-filled a medium.

Political readings include:

Sir Charles Firth, 'The Political Significance of Gulliver's Travels', *Proceedings of the British Academy* 9 (1919–20), pp. 237–59, excerpted in Gravil, 1974

A. E. Case, *Four Essays on Gulliver's Travels*, Princeton University Press, 1945

Ian Higgins, 'Swift's Politics: a Preface to Gulliver's Travels', in Claude Rawson, ed., *Jonathan Swift: a Collection of Critical Essays*, Prentice-Hall, 1995

F. P. Lock, *The Politics of 'Gulliver's Travels'*, Clarendon Press, 1980

J. A. Downie, *Jonathan Swift: Political Writer*, Routledge, 1984

Scientific and Genre studies include:

Marjorie Hope Nicolson and Nora M. Mohler 'The Scientific Background of Swift's Voyage to Laputa', in *Science and Imagination*, Great Seal Books, Ithaca, 1956

Douglas Lane Patey, 'Swift's Satire on "Science" and the Structure of Gulliver's Travels', *ELH* (1991) pp. 809–39, reprinted in Rawson, 1995

Jenny Mecziems, 'The Unity of Swift's "Voyage to Laputa": Structure and Meaning in Utopian Fiction', *Modern Language Review*, 72 (1977), pp. 1–21, in Rawson, 1995

For studies of technique see:

Ricardo Quintana, *The Mind and Art of Jonathan Swift*, 1936, 2nd edition, Methuen, 1953

Ricardo Quintana, *Swift: an Introduction*, Oxford University Press, 1955

John M. Bullitt, *Jonathan Swift and the Anatomy of Satire*, Harvard University Press, 1953

Robert C. Elliott, *The Power of Satire*, Princeton University Press, 1960

Edward W. Rosenheim's *Swift and the Satirist's Art*, University of Chicago Press, 1963

Claude Rawson, ed., *Jonathan Swift: a Collection of Critical Essays*, New Century Views, Prentice-Hall, 1995

HARDLINERS AND SOFTLINERS

In one respect the eighteenth-century debate, between defenders and critics of Swift's treatment of humanity, has never ended. A major battle has been waged in the twentieth century between those who see Swift as delivering a determined assault on human fallibility, from the standpoint of an extreme ascetic (to whom the Houyhnhnms do indeed represent an ideal) and those who feel equally strongly that the entire point of Part IV of *Gulliver's Travels* is to satirise the misanthropy of the satirist. T. O. Wedel, in 1926, argued that Swift, aware of a tendency towards sentimental perfectionism in his era wrote the 'Voyage to the Houyhnhnms' to satirise such forgetfulness of the imperfect nature of mankind. Most modern critics have concluded that the fourth book is not a misanthropic attack on humankind, but a burlesque of the misanthropic Gulliver. John F. Ross (1941), S. H. Monk (1955) and Joseph Horrell (1943) have seen Gulliver as essentially deluded, and eventually deranged, and Kathleen Williams (1958) argued that Swift was fully aware of the inadequacy of 'the life of reason' which he subjects to comic analysis in his final book. Yet it is hard not to feel that Swift shares at least some of Gulliver's animus and disillusion with humanity. R. S. Crane (1962) and James L. Clifford (1974) are among notable critics who have insisted that the message of the work is skewed if we allow the humour to blur the fact that the horses represent a classical ideal of rationality to which Swift was firmly committed, and the Yahoos an angry and tragic vision of human bestiality. Part of the problem in deciding whether the fourth voyage is tragedy or comedy is that in Houyhnhnmland we have nowhere to stand. In Lilliput and Brobdingnag the distortions of scale are relatively easy to negotiate. In Laputa the beings met are recognisably human: the dislocations are in the moral order. In Part IV we have no way of deciding whether the Houyhnhnms or the Yahoos are most 'human', or whether the point is to learn not to identify with either. After all, man is neither Houyhnhnm (pure reason) nor Yahoo (unreason) but, in Swift's own words, *animal rationis capax* – an animal capable of reason, but seemingly incapable of creating a rational order.

If there is a truth about Swift it probably cannot be arrived at by taking the middle line between Thackeray's 'beast' and Arbuthnot's 'merry' Dean. After all, it is not unusual for idealists to feel at times that humanity is so cruel, so irrational, so destructive, that it would be folly to perpetuate it: Gulliver's nausea at having copulated with the Yahoo species and so perpetuated its unreason may not be so far removed from Swift's own feelings about the species in general.

See:

T. O. Wedel, 'On the philosophical background of Gulliver's Travels', *Studies in Philology* 23 (1926) pp. 434–50, and in Gravil, 1974

John F. Ross, 'The Final Comedy of Lemuel Gulliver', *Studies in the Comic*, 8 (1941) pp. 175–96, University of California Publications in English, and in Gravil, 1974

Kathleen Williams, *Jonathan Swift and the Age of Compromise*, University of Kansas Press, 1958

R. S. Crane, 'The Houyhnhnms, the Yahoos and the History of Ideas', in *Reason and Imagination: Studies in the History of Ideas, 1600–1800*, ed. J. A. Mazzeo, Columbia University Press, 1962, and a shorter version in Gravil, 1974

Claude Rawson, *Gulliver and the Gentle Reader*, Routledge, 1973

SWIFT & IRELAND

Swift's relation to Ireland continues to divide critics. One of Claude Rawson's (1995) repeated provocations to other Swift scholars has been his implication that while *A Modest Proposal* is part of Swift's literary services to Ireland, he himself exhibited so much contempt for the native Irish that Sir Charles Firth's reading of the Yahoos as primarily a portrait of 'the savage old Irish' is not far wide of the mark. In *A Modest Proposal* one may choose to see the style as parodying the language of other economic proposers, but the really savage point of the *Proposal* may well be that no saner solution to Ireland's problems was likely to recommend itself to so insane a people. 'In their conception of the Irish as Beasts', Oliver Ferguson (1962) has said, 'Swift and the projector are one'. Other writers, notably Carole Fabricant (1995 and 1982) and Joseph Minns (1991) have placed more emphasis on Swift's experience as a displaced person, in a sort of literary and economic exile, sharing the experience of the colonised. This makes his works available for re-reading with an eye to the dynamics of dispossession and post-colonial experience. In Carole Fabricant's reading, Swift blends the insecurity of 'the scorned Anglo-Irish settler', with 'the frustration and anger of the native Irish population' so that his writings satirise English contempt for Ireland, and repeatedly attack English colonial mythology.

See:

Carole Fabricant, 'Swift as Irish Historian', in *Walking Naboth's Vineyard*, ed. Christopher Fox and Brenda Tooley, University of Notre Dame Press, 1995, and *Swift's Landscape*, Johns Hopkins University Press, 1982

Joseph McMinn, *Jonathan Swift: a Literary Life*, Macmillan, 1991

Oliver Ferguson, *Jonathan Swift and Ireland*, University of Illinois Press, 1962, and the chapter 'The Last Proposals', in Rawson, 1995

THEORETICAL PERSPECTIVES

Swift's work was left remarkably unscathed by the theory-driven modes of criticism which flourished in the 1980s and the 1990s. What were seen as psychoanalytic deformities in the eighteenth and nineteenth centuries have, in the main, been reappraised as proto-Freudian analysis of his culture (Norman O. Brown's famous 1959 essay on Swift's 'excremental vision' argues precisely this and pre-empted what might have been a major industry in amateur psychoanalysis of Swift – in Tuveson, 1964). Moreover, the general fluidity and agility of his writing has kept him proof against the kind of sceptical re-reading of canonical authors practised by **deconstructors** and **new historicists**. Swift's own writings have impelled his better critics to practise varieties of 'reader response criticism' – examining how meaning is made in a constant process of interaction with the text, as we anticipate, stumble, back-track, and re-read – long before that phrase was invented.

Christopher Fox's volume (1995) includes essays in **feminist criticism**, reader response criticism, deconstruction, new historicism, and **psychoanalytic criticism**, and the editor's own thirty-page history of Swift criticism is exemplary. Yet, with the exception of Carole Fabricant's essay on Swift and historicity (not particularly *new* historicist in its procedure), the volume's illustrative essays in contemporary critical approaches add very little to the kind of insight Swift has forced upon his readers throughout the century. Terry Castle's 'deconstructive' essay in Fox's collection (also included in Frank Palmeri's – 1993) illustrates the problem. Instead of deconstructing Swift, Castle attends mainly to Swift's own insights into the problematics of textuality. Inevitably, however, critics have felt impelled to deal directly with such tantalising problems as the negativity one can feel in his representations of women – the sexual innuendoes at the expense of Maids of Honour, the assault on dirt and odours, the disturbing effect of monstrous Brobdingnagian breasts and nipples, the licentiousness of female Yahoos. Oddly, however, Swift seems to have disarmed feminist criticism. His allegedly misogynist poetry can (and probably should) be read as parodic of artificial modes of courtly poetry, and as attacking those who scorn the body. He can be seen as siding with the **realism** of women against the idealism of men, and he clearly admired both Stella and Varina as intellectual beings (he submitted all his writings for the approval of his 'female senate', Lord Orrery said) and advocated equality in education.

The irony-blind, including in this context, D. H. Lawrence, have had great difficulty with such lines of Swift's poetry as these (from 'Strephon and Chloe'):

> Strephon who heard the fuming Rill
> As from a mossy cliff distill;
> Cry'd out, ye Gods, what sound is this?
> Can Chloe, heav'nly Chloe [piss]?

or the closing couplet of 'Cassinus and Peter'

> No wonder how I lost my Wits;
> Oh! Caelia, Caelia, Caelia sh[its].

But a minimal awareness of the eighteenth-century climate of parody, or Swift's general disparagement of those whose vision of humanity could not include our physical realities, or the eighteenth century's taste for the risqué, enables one to see such lines as ironising neither Chloe nor Caelia, but the prurience and pathological idealism of the speakers in the poems. Similarly, while it might be easy enough to demonstrate that Gulliver is misogynist, the mere fact that we never know where Swift stands vis-à-vis Gulliver makes it virtually impossible to sustain a feminist critique of the author. Laura Brown (1990), one critic who does believe that the single most significant theme in Swift's poetry is the attack on women, nevertheless argues that his misogyny is balanced by a surprisingly powerful critique of the racial mythology underlying English colonial expansion.

See:

Christopher Fox, ed., *Jonathan Swift: Gulliver's Travels*, Case Studies in Contemporary Criticism, Bedford Books, Boston, 1995

Christine Rees, 'Gay, Swift and the Nymphs of Drury Lane', *Essays in Criticism* 23 (1973) pp. 1–21, also in Rawson, 1995

Penelope Wilson, 'Feminism and the Augustans: Some Readings and Problems', *Critical Quarterly* 28 (1986) pp. 80–92, also in Rawson, 1995

Terry Castle, 'Why the Houyhnhnms don't write: Swift, Satire and the Fear of the Text', in *Critical Essays on Jonathan Swift*, ed. Frank Palmeri, G. K. Hall, New York, 1993

Margaret Ann Doody, 'Swift among the Women', *Yearbook of English Studies*, 18 (1988) pp. 68–82, also in Palmeri, 1993

Laura Brown, 'Reading Race and Gender', *Eighteenth-Century Studies* 23 (1990) pp. 425–43, also in Palmeri, 1993

FURTHER READING

TEXTS

The Prose Works of Jonathan Swift. Edited by Herbert Davis and others, 16 volumes, Blackwell Publishers, 1939–74.

Volume 11 (1941) is the standard text of the *Travels*.

The Writings of Jonathan Swift. Norton Critical Editions. Edited by Robert A. Greenberg and William Bowman Piper, Norton, 1973

The major and minor prose works, and a good selection of poems and critical essays

Jonathan Swift. The Oxford Authors. Edited by Angus Ross and David Woolley, Oxford University Press, 1984

An attractive compendium of Swift's work

BIOGRAPHY

Ehrenpreis, Irvin, *Swift: The Man, his Works and the Age*. Vol. 1, *Mr Swift and his Contemporaries*. Vol. 2, *Dr Swift*. Vol. 3, *Dean Swift*. Methuen, 1962–83

    The standard, but gigantic, biography

Nokes, David, *Jonathan Swift, a Hypocrite Reversed: a Critical Biography*. Oxford University Press, 1985

    An admirable one-volume biography

Downie, J. A., *Jonathan Swift: Political Writer*, Routledge, 1984

McMinn, Joseph, *Jonathan Swift: a Literary Life*, Macmillan, 1991

    Especially good on the Irish context

CRITICAL ANTHOLOGIES

Donoghue, Denis, *Jonathan Swift: A Critical Anthology*, Penguin, 1971

    A comprehensive collection including Orwell's response to Swift's politics

Foster, Milton P., ed., *A Casebook on Gulliver among the Houyhnhnms*, Crowell, New York, 1961

    The debate on Part IV, up to 1960

Gravil, Richard, ed., *Swift: Gulliver's Travels*, Macmillan, 1974

    A balanced selection of essays depicting changing critical approaches from Firth and Wedel (1919 and 1926), via Herbert Davis and Kathleen Williams (1947, 1958) to Claude Rawson's 'Order and Cruelty', 1970

Palmeri, Frank, *Critical Essays on Jonathan Swift*, G.K. Hall, New York, 1993

Rawson, Claude, ed., *Jonathan Swift: a Collection of Critical Essays*, New Century Views, Prentice-Hall, 1995

    Contains essays by Robert C. Elliott, Penelope Wilson, Ian Higgins, Douglas Patey, Jenny Mecziems, along with A.D. Nuttall on the Houyhnhnms, and Oliver Ferguson on 'The Last Proposals'

Tuveson, Ernest, ed., *Swift: A Collection of Critical Essays*, Twentieth Century Views, Prentice-Hall, 1964

    Still valuable for its inclusion of F.R. Leavis's sceptical revaluation, Norman O. Brown's classic psychoanalytic reading of Swift's 'excremental vision', and Ricardo Quintana's 'Situational Satire'

World events	Author's life	Literary events
		1651 Thomas Hobbes, *Leviathan*
1660 Charles II becomes King		**1660-9** Samuel Pepys writes his diaries
1665 Enactment forbidding sale of Irish cattle, milk, butter and cheese to England		
	1667 Born in Dublin	**1667** John Milton, *Paradise Lost*
1673 Test Act removes Roman Catholics from royal government		
1678 Popish plot		**1678-84** John Bunyan, *The Pilgrim's Progress*
		1682 John Dryden, *Mac Flecknue*
1685 James II accedes to the throne		
		1687 Isaac Newton, *Principia*
1688 Declaration of Indulgence – allows Dissenters and Catholics to worship freely; Glorious Revolution		
1689 William and Mary given crown jointly	**1689** Becomes Secretary to Sir William Temple	
1689-97 War of the League of Augsburg		
1690 Battle of the Boyne		**1690** John Locke, *Two Treatises of Government*
1691 Treaty of Limerick		
	1694 Returns to Ireland	
		1695 William Congreve, *Love for Love*
	1696 Reconciled with Temple and returns to England	
	1697 *The Battle of the Books*	**1697** William Dampier, *A Voyage Around the World*
1699 Enactment forbidding export of woollen goods from Ireland	**1699** Temple dies	
1701-14 War of the Spanish Succession		

World events	Author's life	Literary events
1702 Anne becomes Queen		
1704 Duke of Marlborough wins victory at the Battle of Blenheim	**1704** *Tale of a Tub*	
1707 Kingdoms of Scotland and England unite		
	1710 Assumes editorship of *The Examiner*; begins *Journal to Stella*	
1711 South Sea Bubble	**1711** 'The Conduct of the Allies' (paper)	**1711** Alexander Pope, *Essay on Criticism*
		1712 Alexander Pope, *The Rape of the Lock*
	1713 Appointed Dean of St Patrick's Cathedral, Dublin	
1714 Queen Anne dies; George I accedes		
1715 Jacobite Rebellion		
1716 Septennial Act		
		1719 Daniel Defoe, *Robinson Crusoe*
1721 Robert Walpole appointed First Lord of The Treasury		
	1724-5 *Drapier's Letters* (issued anonymously)	
	1726 *Gulliver's Travels*	
	1729 *A Modest Proposal*	
1739-63 Wars with Spain and War of Austrian Succession		
1745 Second Jacobite Rebellion	**1745** Dies October 19	
		1748 David Hume, *An Enquiry Concerning Human Understanding*; Tobias George Smollett, *The Adventure of Roderick Random*
		1749 Henry Fielding, *Tom Jones*
		1755 Samuel Johnson, *Dictionary of the English Language*

allegory a story which can be read in two ways, for its surface narrative or for the concealed narrative to which the informed reader can penetrate. In the Voyage to Lilliput the surface narrative *allegorises* the history of Augustan politics

allusion a passing reference in a work of literature to something outside itself, whether another literary text, or to legends, historical events and personages

ambiguity the capacity of words and sentences to have double or multiple meanings. In *Gulliver's Travels* the constant presence of allegory and irony means that much of the text must be ambiguous

anaphora (Gk, 'carrying back, repetition') the name for repetition in successive clauses of a word or phrase. Texts 2 and 3 in Textual Analysis contain excellent examples

anagram the mixing up of the letters of a word or phrase to produce another. A lengthy example of 'the anagrammatic method' applied to political espionage is the reading of 'Our brother Tom has just got the piles' as an anagram of 'Resist; a plot is brought home, the tour' (p. 237)

analogue/analogy an analogue is a parallel word or thing or story. Analogical thinking is the basis of some of Swift's satire. If the 'body politic' is sick, analogical thinking may suggest inappropriate remedies, such as an enema, or a tweak on the nose

anatomy in literature, a work offering a detailed dissection of a subject, such as Burton's *The Anatomy of Melancholy* (1621). By analogy one might see *Gulliver's Travels* as 'An Anatomy of Unreason'

Augustan age the period of Swift and his friends is known for its conscious emulation of Roman writers, such as Virgil, Horace and Ovid, in the peaceful and prosperous reign of the Emperor Augustus (27BC–AD14)

deconstruction a critical fashion founded on the gap between signifier (words) and signified (what words refer to). Extreme deconstructionists may deny that texts can ever refer reliably to anything outside themselves. Deconstructive readings tend to replace the search for definitive meaning with the generation of an infinite series of undecidable possibilities

distance a term describing the detachment of the author from what is being said, or the character saying it. Rapid variation in 'distance' between author and speaker is an essential component of irony

Dystopia an unpleasant imagined world; theoretically the opposite of Utopia, though in irony, Utopias can turn into Dystopias

feminist criticism a rapidly expanding set of critical approaches, which when applied to male writing seeks to expose the complicity of literary texts with structures of gender oppression, for instance in the marginalisation or denigration of women, or the employment of language which takes the male to be standard, the female as 'other'

genre the term for a type or division of literature. Poetry, drama and prose fiction are the primary literary genres; but each is divisible into further genres. *Gulliver's Travels* is in prose and is fictional but can be regarded as a novel, or an anatomy, or a Menippean satire

hyperbole use of exaggerated language. A constant feature of irony; whenever Gulliver praises the wisdom and virtue of his country we may suspect hyperbole

image/imagery a hopelessly ambiguous term, covering anything from word-pictures of concrete things (houses, larks, cabbages), or more general ones (gloom, warmth, gaiety), to figures of speech such as simile, metaphor, personification

invective the denunciation of someone or something in a brief or sustained outburst of derogatory or vituperative language. It tends to come into play whenever Swift has lawyers, quacks, or nobles in view

irony (Gk. 'dissembling') a manner of speaking or writing which exploits the gap between what is said and what is meant. In Greek comedy the 'Eiron' pretended to be stupid and naive, while his antagonist, the Alazon, was complacent and boastful. What the Eiron said was understated, its meaning concealed. In fiction, irony exploits the unreliable narrator: we have to work out whether the speaker's perceptions or judgements are to be trusted. The speaker may be quite unironic, a mask for the author's ironic intent

malapropism strictly, the comic use of the wrong or inappropriate word, as by Mrs Malaprop in Sheridan's play *The Rivals* (1775), though there are times in *Gulliver's Travels* when one is left unsure whether Gulliver is guilty of using the wrong words or making them up

mask since Gulliver is not a psychologically consistent character, some critics prefer to refer to him as a mask; or a set or more or less consistent qualities (decent, practical, a bit gullible, trustworthy on the whole) which Swift sometimes wears and sometimes not. Equally, he may speak through other masks in the text; the King of Brobdingnag, or Gulliver's Houyhnhnm master

metaphor the expression of one thing in terms of another: love, Shakespeare claims, in one of his less reliable moments, is 'the star to every wandering bark'. That is, it is so fixed and unchanging that you can navigate by it. In irony we may or may not know whether metaphor is at work. In a sense, since the Voyage to Lilliput is an allegory, the whole of Lilliput is a metaphor for the court of Queen Anne. Certainly 'leaping' and 'creeping' and wiping of posteriors are metaphors for kinds of political behaviour

narrator the teller of a story, or a history. Fictional narrators range from the omniscient to the dysfunctional, and may be dramatised or undramatised. At one end of the scale there may be an impersonal narrator whom we are likely to trust, if only because we have no other viewpoint within the story; at the other a dramatically involved narrator who may be ignorant of some events, prejudiced, or incapable of understanding what is happening. Gulliver is sometimes the soul of truth and honour, and (maybe) as reliable a narrator of tall stories as you ever met; sometimes intensely prejudiced; sometimes wildly wrong

new historicism a reaction against the study of literary texts purely in terms of form. Unlike earlier historicism, which examined literary texts in relation to their historical background, in order to illuminate the author's ideas and values, new historicism tends to be deconstructive in its approach, emphasising the text's exclusions, and blindnesses, and contradictions, and seeing the author as conditioned by 'bourgeois ideology' and incapable of transcending its codes

psychoanalytic criticism a critical approach that tends to see the work of art as the expression of the author's personality, perhaps shaped by unconscious drives and symbolising, involuntarily, what is repressed in the writer's conscious mind

realism/surrealism realism as a literary mode, desirous of creating a faithful picture of reality (or the illusion of reality), began to develop in Swift's time, in such early novels as those of Daniel Defoe. It is very much the creation of the Age of Reason. Surrealism was a phenomenon of the 1920s which emphasised the unconscious and irrational, and preferred dreams and hallucinations as its subject matter. Swift was not a surrealist (he wanted more logic, not less), but his evocations of unreason can look very much like it

satire literature which exhibits or examines vice and folly (or simply ideas or values the writer does not agree with) and makes them appear ridiculous or contemptible. Unlike comedy, which often celebrates human weakness or silliness, satire tends to severity. There are many kinds of satire. Swift's is closest in spirit to Juvenalian satire (Juvenal was a Roman poet, AD60–130), scourging mankind for its errors; and in form to Mennipean satire (named after Menippus, a Greek cynic of the third century BC). Menippean satire is formally heterogeneous (using narratives, dialogues, parables, digressions, lists, etc) and tends to depict mental attitudes rather than characters

theme the central ideas of a work, such as, in this case, human pride and irrationality

tone a literary text usually supposes a speaker; and understanding that speaker is a matter of catching, from textual clues, whether something is said seriously, gently, playfully, ironically, savagely. In an ironic text two tones (Gulliver's and Swift's) may be at work at once or in very close juxtaposition

Utopia both an ideal place (in Greek 'outopia' means 'no place') and a literary work treating such a place. Sir Thomas More's *Utopia* (1516) depicted an ideal commonwealth. The opposite of Utopia is Dystopia, such as Aldous Huxley's ironically named future fantasy, *Brave New World* (1932)

Author of this note

Richard Gravil has taught at the University of Victoria, B.C., the University of Lódź, Poland, the University of Otago and The College of St Mark and St John in Plymouth. His publications include work on Swift, Coleridge, Wordsworth, Dickens and Lawrence, and *Romantic Dialogues: Anglo-American Continuities, 1776–1862* (St Martin's Press, 2000).

York Notes Advanced (£3.99 each)

Margaret Atwood
Cat's Eye

Margaret Atwood
The Handmaid's Tale

Jane Austen
Mansfield Park

Jane Austen
Persuasion

Jane Austen
Pride and Prejudice

Alan Bennett
Talking Heads

William Blake
Songs of Innocence and of Experience

Charlotte Brontë
Jane Eyre

Emily Brontë
Wuthering Heights

Angela Carter
Nights at the Circus

Geoffrey Chaucer
The Franklin's Prologue and Tale

Geoffrey Chaucer
The Miller's Prologue and Tale

Geoffrey Chaucer
Prologue To the Canterbury Tales

Geoffrey Chaucer
The Wife of Bath's Prologue and Tale

Samuel Taylor Coleridge
Selected Poems

Joseph Conrad
Heart of Darkness

Daniel Defoe
Moll Flanders

Charles Dickens
Great Expectations

Charles Dickens
Hard Times

Emily Dickinson
Selected Poems

John Donne
Selected Poems

Carol Ann Duffy
Selected Poems

George Eliot
Middlemarch

George Eliot
The Mill on the Floss

T.S. Eliot
Selected Poems

F. Scott Fitzgerald
The Great Gatsby

E.M. Forster
A Passage to India

Brian Friel
Translations

Thomas Hardy
The Mayor of Casterbridge

Thomas Hardy
The Return of the Native

Thomas Hardy
Selected Poems

Thomas Hardy
Tess of the d'Urbervilles

Seamus Heaney
Selected Poems from Opened Ground

Nathaniel Hawthorne
The Scarlet Letter

Kazuo Ishiguro
The Remains of the Day

Ben Jonson
The Alchemist

James Joyce
Dubliners

John Keats
Selected Poems

Christopher Marlowe
Doctor Faustus

Arthur Miller
Death of a Salesman

John Milton
Paradise Lost Books I & II

Toni Morrison
Beloved

Sylvia Plath
Selected Poems

Alexander Pope
Rape of the Lock and other poems

William Shakespeare
Antony and Cleopatra

William Shakespeare
As You Like It

William Shakespeare
Hamlet

William Shakespeare
King Lear

William Shakespeare
Measure for Measure

William Shakespeare
The Merchant of Venice

William Shakespeare
A Midsummer Night's Dream

William Shakespeare
Much Ado About Nothing

William Shakespeare
Othello

William Shakespeare
Richard II

William Shakespeare
Romeo and Juliet

William Shakespeare
The Taming of the Shrew

William Shakespeare
The Tempest

William Shakespeare
Twelfth Night

William Shakespeare
The Winter's Tale

George Bernard Shaw
Saint Joan

Mary Shelley
Frankenstein

Jonathan Swift
Gulliver's Travels and A Modest Proposal

Alfred, Lord Tennyson
Selected Poems

Alice Walker
The Color Purple

Oscar Wilde
The Importance of Being Earnest

Tennessee Williams
A Streetcar Named Desire

John Webster
The Duchess of Malfi

Virginia Woolf
To the Lighthouse

W.B. Yeats
Selected Poems

FUTURE TITLES IN THE YORK NOTES SERIES

Jane Austen
Emma

Jane Austen
Sense and Sensibility

Samuel Beckett
Waiting for Godot and
Endgame

Louis de Bernières
Captain Corelli's Mandolin

Charlotte Brontë
Villette

Caryl Churchill
Top Girls and *Cloud Nine*

Charles Dickens
Bleak House

T.S. Eliot
The Waste Land

Thomas Hardy
Jude the Obscure

Homer
The Iliad

Homer
The Odyssey

Aldous Huxley
Brave New World

D.H. Lawrence
Selected Poems

Christopher Marlowe
Edward II

George Orwell
Nineteen Eighty-four

Jean Rhys
Wide Sargasso Sea

William Shakespeare
Henry IV Pt I

William Shakespeare
Henry IV Part II

William Shakespeare
Macbeth

William Shakespeare
Richard III

Tom Stoppard
Arcadia and *Rosencrantz and
Guildenstern are Dead*

Virgil
The Aeneid

Jeanette Winterson
*Oranges are Not the Only
Fruit*

Tennessee Williams
Cat on a Hot Tin Roof

Metaphysical Poets

GCSE and equivalent levels (£3.50 each)

Maya Angelou
I Know Why the Caged Bird Sings

Jane Austen
Pride and Prejudice

Alan Ayckbourn
Absent Friends

Elizabeth Barrett Browning
Selected Poems

Robert Bolt
A Man for All Seasons

Harold Brighouse
Hobson's Choice

Charlotte Brontë
Jane Eyre

Emily Brontë
Wuthering Heights

Shelagh Delaney
A Taste of Honey

Charles Dickens
David Copperfield

Charles Dickens
Great Expectations

Charles Dickens
Hard Times

Charles Dickens
Oliver Twist

Roddy Doyle
Paddy Clarke Ha Ha Ha

George Eliot
Silas Marner

George Eliot
The Mill on the Floss

Anne Frank
The Diary of Anne Frank

William Golding
Lord of the Flies

Oliver Goldsmith
She Stoops To Conquer

Willis Hall
The Long and the Short and the Tall

Thomas Hardy
Far from the Madding Crowd

Thomas Hardy
The Mayor of Casterbridge

Thomas Hardy
Tess of the d'Urbervilles

Thomas Hardy
The Withered Arm and other Wessex Tales

L.P. Hartley
The Go-Between

Seamus Heaney
Selected Poems

Susan Hill
I'm the King of the Castle

Barry Hines
A Kestrel for a Knave

Louise Lawrence
Children of the Dust

Harper Lee
To Kill a Mockingbird

Laurie Lee
Cider with Rosie

Arthur Miller
The Crucible

Arthur Miller
A View from the Bridge

Robert O'Brien
Z for Zachariah

Frank O'Connor
My Oedipus Complex and Other Stories

George Orwell
Animal Farm

J.B. Priestley
An Inspector Calls

J.B. Priestley
When We Are Married

Willy Russell
Educating Rita

Willy Russell
Our Day Out

J.D. Salinger
The Catcher in the Rye

William Shakespeare
Henry IV Part 1

William Shakespeare
Henry V

William Shakespeare
Julius Caesar

William Shakespeare
Macbeth

William Shakespeare
The Merchant of Venice

William Shakespeare
A Midsummer Night's Dream

William Shakespeare
Much Ado About Nothing

William Shakespeare
Romeo and Juliet

William Shakespeare
The Tempest

William Shakespeare
Twelfth Night

George Bernard Shaw
Pygmalion

Mary Shelley
Frankenstein

R.C. Sherriff
Journey's End

Rukshana Smith
Salt on the Snow

John Steinbeck
Of Mice and Men

Robert Louis Stevenson
Dr Jekyll and Mr Hyde

Jonathan Swift
Gulliver's Travels

Robert Swindells
Daz 4 Zoe

Mildred D. Taylor
Roll of Thunder, Hear My Cry

Mark Twain
Huckleberry Finn

James Watson
Talking in Whispers

Edith Wharton
Ethan Frome

William Wordsworth
Selected Poems

A Choice of Poets

Mystery Stories of the Nineteenth Century including The Signalman

Nineteenth Century Short Stories

Poetry of the First World War

Six Women Poets

Notes